Peter O'Leary

Mion-Caint

An Easy Irish Phrase Book

Peter O'Leary

Mion-Caint
An Easy Irish Phrase Book

ISBN/EAN: 9783337120993

Printed in Europe, USA, Canada, Australia, Japan

Cover: Foto ©Paul-Georg Meister /pixelio.de

More available books at **www.hansebooks.com**

ᵐꞮᴏꞃ - Ċᴀꞽꞃꞇ

—:o:—

AN EASY

IRISH PHRASE BOOK.

COMPILED

FOR THE GAELIC LEAGUE

BY

THE REV. PETER O'LEARY, P.P.

Dublin:

PUBLISHED BY THE GAELIC LEAGUE,

24 UPPER O'CONNELL STREET.

1899.

PREFACE.

My mind has been much exercised for some time over the position of persons who are anxious to learn Irish. There are two classes who wish to learn, viz., those who can speak Irish and those who cannot. Those who can speak it wish to learn to read it. Those who can neither speak nor read it wish to learn both. For the use of both classes there is nothing available but Father O'Growney's little books.

The *Gaelic Journal* is a splendid publication. There is more solid erudition within its small compass than within the compass of any English Journal twenty times its size. But it is only useful to learners when they have acquired a fairly good knowledge of the language. Even the grammatical and critical matter which is contained in it is not appreciated by those who do not know Irish. No one has ever yet learned a language from its grammar. In fact, a person must know the language before he can understand the grammar.

Then what about the other Irish matter which can be had in those volumes whose contents have been taken from the works of Irish writers of Keating's age?

I have to state as a positive fact, that, as far as
learners are concerned, whether they be learners who
can already speak Irish, or learners who cannot, those
volumes are many degrees worse than useless. The
very first page of any of these books, and I say it from
positive experience, is enough to frighten even a
fluent Irish speaker from any further effort at be-
coming an Irish reader, unless he be a person of iron
determination. Fortunately we have in considerable
abundance people of that stamp. Persons whom even
a sensation like intermittent lock-jaw cannot frighten
from the work. But when a fluent Irish speaker,
whose native Irish vocabulary is overflowing with
wealth, and whose organs of speech can use that
vocabulary like rolling music, when he, I say, looks at
the page of an Ossianic society volume, and finds him-
self threatened with lock-jaw almost at every sentence,
he naturally comes to the conclusion that there is
something wrong. He does not know what is wrong,
but he lays down the volume.

The learner who never *spoke* a word of Irish is in a
far worse plight. He does not *suspect* that there is
anything wrong. He struggles onward through the
Easy Lessons, through the Ossianic volume, lock-jaw
and all. Then he gets among the people, and lo ! *not
a syllable of the people's language can he understand.*

What *is* it that is wrong ? There are a good many
things wrong, but the whole evil can be reduced to
this one fact. For a living language, the books and
the speech of the people *should go hand in hand.*
What is printed in the books should be the exact
representation of what comes out of the people's

mouths. The Irish of our Ossianic books is of course not essentially different from the Irish which I speak. But if I were to meet my neighbours *who do not read Irish;* and if I were to speak to them in the Ossianic style, matters would soon come to a dead lock.

Why not give the people their own speech! That is what is wrong. What would be the result if a person who can speak English and who wishes to learn to read it, were to have an unmodernised copy of Bacon placed in his hand? He would learn his book-lesson, but he would find that it would set his neighbours laughing at him. It would effectually prevent that man from learning to read. Suppose him a person who knows no English at all, what is his position? It is exactly that of the Irish learner who *knows no Irish at all,* and who is floundering through an Ossianic book.

The position of those two classes of Irish learners has been a trouble to me for a long time. In order to try and do something to remedy the evil I have written the following phrase-book.

In constructing it I have made it a point not only to give in the phrases the living language of the people as far as syntax and style of speech is concerned, but also to strip the individual words, as far as possible, of the encumbrances with which centuries of neglect must have naturally incrusted their written forms. It is these incrustations that paralyse the efforts of the book-learner. It is the total absence of them that makes the spoken language so smooth.

For example; everybody has heard of the *rule* called ᴄᴀᴏᴸ ᴸᴇ ᴄᴀᴏᴸ. Now as a matter of fact this is

not a rule. It is a phonetic *truth*. It is a truth
which belongs to the nature of Irish speech. Accord-
ing to the nature of Irish speech a consonant cannot
be sounded broad if it be in contact with a slender
vowel. And again, the moment a consonant has become slender a broad vowel cannot continue in contact
with it. Take for example the word ᴄᴀᴛ. If the
diminutive -ín is to be added to it the ᴛ becomes
slender on account of the ı of -ín. Then, because the
ᴛ has become slender, the preceding broad ᴀ cannot
remain in contact with it. *The organs of speech, to
the distinct knowledge and cognizance of the ear*, in-
troduce a slight ı-sound before the ᴛ.

It is not a *rule*. It is a *natural law* of Irish arti-
culation. That law is as vigorous now in the spoken
Irish as ever it was. It was not made by scholars,
nor by bards, nor by grammarians. It belongs by
nature to the language. It must be admitted that the
thought of introducing it into the spelling of the
words was a magnificent thought. It has been a most
fortunate thing for us and for our language that the
ears of our fathers were so good, and that they gave
us the result in black and white. Had they not done
so, and had our language ceased to be spoken without
any person's having called attention to that law, the
knowledge of its existence would have been lost.

But the principle has been fearfully abused. It
has been looked upon as a mere spelling-rule. The
result has been that writers, without any regard to
the *ear*, have merely followed the *eye*. They have
acted as a person would act who, instead of ᴄᴀıᴛín,
would write ᴄᴀᴛᴀoín. The latter form observes the

"*rule*," but there is danger of lock-jaw in trying to
pronounce it, even for a habitual Irish speaker. Such
writers have insisted upon observing the "rule" no
matter how many consonants may come between the
two vowels. They will, for example, write buaɪlreaṗ.
I have never heard that word out of any person's
mouth. I have always heard buaɪlṗaṗ. But I *have*
heard buaɪlceaṗ, not buaɪlcaṗ. I have never heard
cuiḃeaṗaċ, but always cuiḃṗaċ.

It will not be easy to get rid of these incrustations
all of a sudden. In fact it would be dangerous. All
the pruning should not be done at once. Still there
is no harm in making a beginning. That beginning
should be made, taking the *ear* as guide. The principle in question belongs exclusively to the ear. It
has nothing whatever to do with the orthography of
the language.

There are several other things which require clipping.
I have never heard ɒeɪṗeaḃ = *end*, but always ɒeɪṗe.
I have never heard aɪʒneaḃ = *mind*, but always aɪʒne.
Am I expected to go on writing what I have never
heard ? I have always heard distinctly the "nn" at
the end of such words as ʒann = *scarce*, ṗann = *weak*,
but I have never heard it at the end of the third
person singular of a verb. Then why should I write
into the word a sound which I have never heard there ?

Then what of the authority of the past ? In the
first place I don't give much for the authority of
people who turned a phonetic law into a spelling-rule.
In the second place, if we go back as far as true
authority we find that those double letters were then
distinctly heard—nn and nɒ were written one for the

8 PREFACE.

other, and ꞃꞃ was sounded like the present ꞃꞇ. I have
myself distinctly heard ꞇoꞃꞃᴀꝺ pronounced ꞇoꞃꞇᴀꝺ.

In the following pages, as a step towards the simpli-
fication of our spelling, the use of double consonants
is omitted when possible. Such an omission is of
course impossible in such words as ᵹᴀnn (*scarce*), ꝼᴀnn
(*weak*), etc., because the effect of the omission would
be to produce other words with both a different sound
and a different meaning.

The reader is to take it for granted that the sound
represented by "nn" is quite different from that
represented by "n."

With regard to "ꞃꞃ," it has been found necessary
to avoid it altogether. It is always equivalent either
to "ꞃ" or to "ꞃꞇ." Hence "ꞃ" or "ꞃꞇ" have been
substituted for it in the following pages.

The chief purpose of this First Part is to teach the
syntax which regulates the use of the two link-words
"ꞃ" and "ꞇᴊ."

A Second Part is to follow, which will illustrate in
copious detail the forms and uses of the Irish verb.
Also a Third Part, which will deal with the syntax of
those words which express relation.

The learner may rest assured that *not a single word
or phrase has been invented*. They are all, without
exception, actual living speech. There is not an
Irish-speaking old person in Munster who would not
understand every word and every phrase at once.
Still the learner will find the syntax throughout most
perfect, and most rigidly adhered to, in such a manner
that he cannot fail to be astounded when he remem-
bers that this wonderfully symmetrical phraseology

has been for centuries the every day dialogue of millions of people who could neither read nor write.

For example; in the whole range of the language there is not a single exception to the rule which says that " ᵼ " takes the predicate next to it, and that " cá " takes the subject next to it. Now, in English common conversation there are hundreds of instances in the use of the verb *to be*, in which no person can tell which of the two nominative cases is the subject.

That is only one out of the numberless beauties which await the learner.

A most useful exercise for the learner will be, after having mastered the meaning of each phrase, to take it asunder, and to distinguish carefully the link-word, the subject or nominative case, and the predicate, that is the piece of *information* which is given concerning the subject. Thus :—

ᵼ aınṁiʒe bó = A cow is an animal.

ᵼ, the link; bó, the subject; aınṁiʒe, the information given regarding the cow.

Cá an bó 'na ṗeaṗaṁ = The cow is standing.

Cá, the link; an bó, the subject; 'na ṗeaṗaṁ, the information given.

ᵼ 'na ṗeaṗaṁ acá an bó = It is standing the cow is.
ᵼ, the link; acá an bó, the subject; 'na ṗeaṗaṁ, the information which is given regarding the *position in which the cow is.*

(Oeiṗim) ʒuṗ bó i = (I say) that she is a cow. ʒuṗ, the link; i, the subject; bó, the information given regarding i.

peaoaṗ ua Laoʒaiṗe.

ꝏꝃ--Ċꝏ

"ꞮS" ᴀɴᴅ "Ꞇꙋ."

I. "Ɪꞃ," or any part of it, is the link between two
substantives, or between two modes, as "Ɪꞃ
ꙇꙇꙇꙇꙇꙅe ꝃꝏ"; "Ɪꞃ 'ꙇꙇ ꝃeꙅꙇꙇꙇ ꙇꝁꙋ ꝃꞮ."

II. "Ꞇꙋ," or any part of it, is the link between a
substantive and any of its modes, as "ꞇꙋ ꙇꙇ
ꝃꝏ 'ꙇꙇ ꝃeꙅꙇꙇꙇ"; "ꞇꙋ ꝃꞮ ꙇꙅ ꝃꙋꝃꙋꙇ."

III. The *predicate* comes next to "Ɪꞃ," the *subject*
comes next to "Ꞇꙋ." "ꙏꞇꙋ" is the relative
form of "Ꞇꙋ." "Ɪꞃ" can be very often
omitted.

PHRASES

Present Time.

Iᵷ bᵲeᴣᵹ ᴀn lᴀ́ é.	It is a *fine* day.
Iᵷ lᴀ́ bᵲeᴣᵹ é.	It is a fine day.
Iᵷ ᵹeᴀᵲ lᴀ́ᵼᴅᵼᵲ é.	He is a strong man.
Iᵷ lᴀ́ᵼᴅᵼᵲ ᴀn ᵹeᴀᵲ é.	He is a *strong* man.
Iᵷ é ᴀn ᵹeᴀᵲ lᴀ́ᵼᴅᵼᵲ é.	He *is* a *strong* man.
Iᵷ lᴀ́ᵼᴅᵼᵲ ᴀᴄᴀ́ ᵲé.	He IS *strong*.
Ṅᴀ́ᴄ lᴀ́ᵼᴅᵼᵲ ᴀᴄᴀ́ ᵲé !	How strong he is ! (Lit., Isn't it strong he is !)
Ꞇᴀ́ ᵲé lᴀᵹ.	He is weak.
Ꞇᴀ́ ᵲé ᵹo lᴀᵹ.	He IS *weak*.
Iᵷ lᴀᵹ ᴀᴄᴀ́ ᵲé.	He is very weak.
Ꞇᴀ́ ᵲé ᴀnᴀ lᴀᵹ.	He is *very* weak.
Ꞇᴀ́ ᵲé ᵹo h-ᴀnᴀ lᴀᵹ.	He IS *very* weak.
Ꞇᴀ́ ᵲé ᵹo h-ᴀnᴀ lᴀᵹ ᴀᵲᵹᴀᴅ.	He is very weak entirely.
Ꞇᴀ́ ᴀn ᴅonᴀᵲ le lᴀᵼᵹe ᴀᵼᵲ.	He is excessively weak.
Iᵷ ᵹeᴀᵲ Ṁᵼᴄel.	Michael is a man.
Iᵷ ᵹeᴀᵲ mᴀᵼᴄ Ṁᵼᴄel.	Michael is a good man.
Iᵷ ᵹeᴀᵲ ᵹᴀn ṁᴀᵼᴄ Ṁᵼᴄel.	Michael is a useless man.
Iᵷ ᵹeᴀᵲ meᴀᴄᴄᴀ é.	He is a good-for-nothing man.
ᵹeᴀᵲ meᴀᴄᴄᴀ.	A man who is a failure.
Ꞇᴀ́ Ꞇᴀᴅᵹ ᵼ n' ᵹeᴀᵲ.	Thade is a man.
Ꞇᴀ́ ᵲé ᵼ n' ᵹeᴀᵲ ṁóᵲ.	He is a big man.
Ꞇᴀ́ ᵲé ᵼ n' ᵹeᴀᵲ ḃeᴀᵹ.	He is a little man.

Iγ ᴅᴩoċ ᴅuıne é.	He is a bad man.
Iγ ᴅuıne ᴩóᵹɑnᴄɑ é.	He is a good man, *i.e.*, he is a man who does good to others.
Iγ ᴄɑʟɑṁ ᴩóᵹɑnᴄɑ é.	It is good land, *i.e.*, kind, productive land.
Iγ ᴄɑıʟʟᴄe ɑn ᴄɑʟɑṁ é.	It is dreadfully bad land.
Iγ ᴄɑıʟʟᴄe ɑn ɑıṁᴩıᴩ í.	It is terrible weather.
Iγ ᴄɑıʟʟᴄe ɑn ʟá é.	It is a frightful day.
Iγ ᴄɑıʟʟᴄe ɑn ʟá é ʟe ᴩʟıċe.	It is a frightful day, it is so wet.
Iγ ᴄɑıʟʟᴄe ɑ ᴅeınıᴩ oᴩm é.	You *have* treated me scurvily.
Iγ ᴅeɑᴩ ɑn ʙuɑċɑıʟ ᴄu !	You are a nice boy !
Iγ mɑıᴄ ɑn ᴄᴩuɑıʟ ɑᵹɑᴄ é!	You have done well !
Ní mıᴅe ᴃeıᴄ ɑᵹ ʙᴩɑᴄ oᴩᴄ !	It is no harm to be depending on you !
Ní h-eɑᴅ ᵹo ᴅeıṁın.	No indeed.
Ní ᴄʟoċ ıɑᴩɑn.	Iron is not stone.
Ní h-ɑᴅmɑᴅ ᴄʟoċ.	Stone is not wood.
Ní ᴩeóıʟ ɑᴅmɑᴅ.	Wood is not flesh.
Ní ᴄnáṁ ɑᴅɑᴩᴄ.	Horn is not bone.
Ní ᴩıonɑ ᴄᴩoıceɑn.	Skin is not hair.
Ní ʟeɑᴄɑᴩ ᴩıonɑ.	Hair is not leather.
Ní ᴩuıʟ uıᴩᵹe.	Water is not blood.
Ní h-uıᴩᵹe ʙɑınne.	Milk is not water.
Ní ʙɑınne ʙıoᴄáıʟe.	Spirit is not milk.
Ní ᵹɑınıṁ ᴄᴩé.	Earth is not sand.
Ní ᴄᴩé ᵹɑınıṁ.	Sand is not earth.
Ní ᵹɑınıṁ ᵹᴩeɑn.	Gravel is not sand.
Ní ᵹᴩeɑn ᵹɑınıṁ.	Sand is not gravel
Ní móın ᵹuɑʟ.	Coal is not turf.

Ní ʒuaL móin. — Turf is not coal.
Ní ⱁuiLleabaṗ ḟéuṗ. — Grass is not foliage.
Ní cṗann cabáiṛce. — A cabbage is not a tree.
Ní cabáiṛce cṗann. — A tree is not a cabbage.
Ní cabáiṛce ḟeóiL. — Meat is not cabbage.
Ní ḟeóiL cabáiṛce. — Cabbage is not meat.
Ní plúṗ min. — Meal is not flour.
Ní min plúṗ. — Flour is not meal.
Ní bó capaL. — A horse is not a cow.
Ní capaL bó. — A cow is not a horse.
Ní ʒaṁuin ṛioṗaċ. — A foal is not a calf.
Ní ṛioṗaċ capaL. — A horse is not a foal.
Ní ʒoṛc ʒaṛaiⱁ. — A garden is not a corn-field.

Ní cṗuiċneaċc óṛna. — Barley is not wheat.
Ní coiṗce cṗuiċneaċc. — Wheat is not oats.
Ní ⱁaiṛ ʒiúiṛ. — Fir is not oak.
Ní ḟuinṛeóʒ coLL. — Hazel is not ash.
Ní miṛe Caⱁʒ. — I am not Tim.
Ní Caⱁʒ miṛe. — My name is not Tim.
An aⱁmaⱁ cloċ? — { Is stone wood ? / Is a stone wood ? }
An bóċaṛ coṛán? — Is a path a road ?
An ḟeaṛ Caⱁʒ? — Is Tim a man ?
An capaL bó? — Is a cow a horse ?
An bó capaL? — Is a horse a cow ?
An amáṛaċ an ⱁóṁnaċ? — Is to-morrow Sunday ? (Lit., Is the Sunday to-morrow ?)

An í an aoine acá aʒainn? — Is to-day Friday ?
An é an Saċaṛn acá aʒainn? — Is to-day Saturday ?

An indiu an Luan ?	Is this Monday ?
An é an Luan atá indiu againn ?	Is this Monday ?
An é ṡeo an Luan ?	Is this Monday ?
An file tuṗa ?	Are *you* a poet ?
An gaḃaṗ mionán ?	Is a kid a goat ?
An muc maoṗa ?	Is a dog a pig ?
An maoṗa muc ?	Is a pig a dog ?
An leat-ṗa an ṁuc ?	Is the pig *yours* ?
An leat an gaḃaṗ ?	Is the dog yours ?
An leat an maoiṗín ?	Is the little dog yours ?
An tu a ċaill é ?	Was it you that lost him ?
An tu a ḟuaiṗ é ?	Was it you that found him ?
An tu a tug leat é ?	Was it you brought him ?
An tu d'ḟág anṗó é ?	Was it you left him here ?
An dóiċ leat guṗ leat é ?	Do you think he is yours ?
An mbéaṗṡaiṗ leat é ?	Will you take him with you ?
An ḃfágṡaiṗ ad ḋiaig é ?	Will you leave him behind ?
An dtaḃaṗṡaiṗ dóṁṡa é ?	Will you give him to *me* ?
An coileán mait é ?	Is he a good pup ?
An mianaċ mait é ?	Is he a good breed ?
An dṗoċ ṁianaċ é ?	Is he a bad breed ?
An mianaċ ḟóganta é ?	Is he a good breed ?
An ḃfuil foluiġeaċt ann ?	Is he highly bred ?
An cáḃóg é ?	Is he a low-bred cur ?
An ndíolṗá é ?	Would you sell him ?
An gceannóċṗá é ?	Would you buy him ?
An móṗ a ḃeiḋeaḋ uait aiṗ ?	How much would you be asking for him ?

An móṗ aṙ a nṁíoúṗa é ?	For how much would you sell him ?
An móṗ aṙ a ḃṙaiġinn uaic é ?	For how much would I get him from you ?
An móṗ a ceanócaḋ uaic é?	How much would buy him from you ?
An móṗ a coṙnócaḋ ṙé ?	How much would he cost ?
An 'mó bliaġain é ?	How many years old is he ?
An 'mó lá é ?	How many days old is he ?
An 'mó mí é ?	How many months old is he ?
An 'mó ṙáice é?	How many quarters (of a year) old is he ?
An 'mó ṙeaccṁain é ?	How many weeks old is he ?
An 'mó ṙiacal aiġe ?	How many teeth has he ?
An 'mó ṙúil ann ?	How many eyes has he ?
An 'mó eaṙbal aiṙ ?	How many tails has he ?
An 'mó ceann aiṙ ?	How many heads has he ?
An 'mó coṙ ṙé ?	How many legs has he ?
An 'mó coṙ coṙaiġ ṙé ?	How many fore legs has he ?
An 'mó coṙ ṁeiṙiḋ ṙé ?	How many hind legs has he ?
An 'mó iunġa aiṙ ?	How many claws has he ?
An leac ṙéin é ?	Is he your own ?
An aṁlaiḋ a ġuiṁiṙ é ?	Is it how you stole him ?
An aṁlaiḋ a ceanuiġiṙ é?	Is it how you bought him ?
An aṁlaiḋ a ṙuaṙaiṙ aġ ḋul amú é ?	Is it how you found him losing ?

An amlaiḋ do ḃronaḋ ort é?	Is it how some one made you a present of him?
Is amlaiḋ do rugaḋ agus do tógaḋ agam féin é.	It is how he was born and reared in my own possession.
An dáiríriḃ ataoi?	Are you in earnest? (Lit., Is it in earnest you are?)
Is dáiríriḃ.	Yes, I am. (Lit., Yes, it is in earnest [I am]).
Naċ breáġ an lá é!	Isn't it a fine day!
Naċ fliuċ an lá é!	Isn't it a wet day!
Naċ fuar an lá é!	Isn't it a cold day!
Naċ teiṫ an lá é!	Isn't it a hot day!
Naċ moċ atá sé!	How very early it is! (Lit., Isn't it early it is!)
Naċ áluinn é!	Isn't it grand!
Naċ breáġ é!	Isn't it beautiful!
Naċ breáġ atá sé!	Isn't it beautiful!
Naċ bog atá sé!	How soft it is! (Lit., Isn't it soft it is!)
Naċ bog atá sé agat!	How soft you have it!
Naċ bog atá do ċroiceann ort!	How soft your skin is upon you!
Naċ bog a ṫagan caint ċugat!	How easy talk comes to you!
Naċ cruaiḋ atá an fiona air!	How hard the hair is upon him!
Naċ fada ataoi leis!	How long you are at it!
Naċ é Taḋg é?	Is it not Thade?
Naċ mac duit é?	Is he not a son of yours?
Naċ é do ṁac é?	Is he not your son?
Naċ é do ṁac féin é?	Is he not your own son?

Nác é do ṁac-ṗa é?	Is he not *your* son?
Nác é do ṁac-ṗa ṗéin é?	Is he not actually *your* own son?
Nác mac duiṫṗe ṗéin é?	Is he not actually a son to yourself?
Nác bean í?	Is she not a woman?
Nác í do bean í?	Is she not your wife?
Nác í ṗin í?	Is not that she?
Nác í ṗin ṗéin í?	Is not that she exactly?
Nác í ṗin í ṗéin?	Is not that herself?
Nác leaṫ í?	Is she not yours?
Nác leaṫ-ṗa í?	Is she not *yours*?
Nác í t'inġean í?	Is she not your daughter?
Nác inġean duiṫ í?	Is she not a daughter of yours?
Nác inġean duiṫ-ṗe í?	Is she not a daughter of *yours*?
Nác í t'inġean-ṗa í?	Is she not your daughter?
Nác inġean duiṫ ṗéin í?	Is she not a daughter of your own?
Nác í t'inġean ṗéin í?	Is she not your own daughter?
Nác í ṗin do ṗġian?	Is not that your knife?
Nác í do ṗġian í?	Is it not your knife?
Nác í do ṗġian ṗéin í?	Is it not your own knife?
Nác leaṫ í?	Does it not belong to you?
Nác ṗġian leaṫ í?	Is it not a knife of yours?
Nác ṗġian leaṫṗa í?	Is it not a knife of *yours*?
Nác í do ċuid ṗéin í?	Is it not your own property?
Nác leaṫ ṗéin í?	Does it not belong to yourself?

B

Ⅱác ⚇u ⚇n ⚇eⰑ⚇!	What a man you are !
Ⅱác é ⚇n ⚇eⰑ⚇ é ! ⚇ nⰑu-ⰑⰑⰑⰑ ÉⰑmon ⰑeⰑⰑ ⚇n ⚇eⰑⰑe.	What a man he is ! as Ned said to the ram.

Past Time.

ⰑⰑ ⰑíⰑ ⰑⰑⰑⰑn.	Brian was a king.
ⰑⰑ ⰑíⰑ ⚇⚇ⰑⰑⰑ é.	He was a noble king.
ⰑⰑ ⰑⰑⰑc ⚇ó ⅯⰑⰑcⰑⰑ.	Morgan was a son of his.
ⰑⰑ ⰑóⰑ ⚇n ⰑíⰑ é.	He was a *great* king.
ⰑⰑ cóⰑⰑⰑⰑⰑⰑ ⚇n ⰑíⰑ é.	He was a *powerful* king.
ⰑⰑ ⰑíⰑ cóⰑⰑⰑⰑⰑⰑ é.	He was a powerful king.
ⰑíⰑ cóⰑⰑⰑⰑⰑⰑ ⚇oⰑ eⰑⰑ é.	He *was* a powerful king.
ⰑⰑ ⰑⰑⰑⰑ ⚇n ⚇eⰑⰑ é.	He was a good man.
⚇eⰑⰑ mⰑⰑⰑ ⚇oⰑ eⰑⰑ é.	He *was* a good man.
⚇oⰑ ⚇oíⰑⰑnn ⚇n ⰑⰑ é.	It was a *splendid* day.
ⰑⰑ ⚇oíⰑⰑnn ⚇oⰑ eⰑⰑ é.	It *was* a splendid day.
ⰑⰑ ⚇ⰑⰑⰑ ⚇n ⰑⰑ é.	It was a dry day.
ⰑⰑ ⚇nⰑ ⚇ⰑⰑⰑ ⚇oⰑ eⰑⰑ é.	It was a *very dry* day.
ⰑⰑ ⰑⰑ ⰑⰑoⰑⰑⰑⰑⰑ é.	It was a warm day.
ⰑⰑ ⰑⰑ ⚇nⰑ ⰑⰑoⰑⰑⰑⰑⰑ é.	It was a *very warm* day.
ⰑⰑ ⚇nⰑ ⰑⰑoⰑⰑⰑⰑⰑ ⚇oⰑ eⰑⰑ é.	It *was* a very warm day.
ⰑⰑ ⰑóⰑ ⚇n ⰑⰑoⰑⰑⰑ é.	It was great heat.
ⰑⰑ ⰑⰑⰑoⰑⰑ ⚇n ⚇eⰑⰑ é.	He was a *strong* man.
⚇eⰑⰑ ⚇nⰑ ⰑⰑⰑoⰑⰑ⚇oⰑ eⰑⰑ é.	He was a *very* strong man.
Ⱁ' é ⚇eⰑⰑ ⰑⰑ ⚇ⰑeⰑⰑe ⚇Ⱁ ⚇ cⰑneⰑⰑ é.	He was the strongest man of his race.
Ⱁ' é ⰑⰑ ⰑⰑⰑⰑ ⰑeⰑnn ⚇Ⱁ ⰑⰑⰑⰑ⚇.	It was he that least felt the cold.
Ⱁ' é ⰑⰑ ⰑⰑⰑ ⰑéⰑⰑⰑⰑⰑ ⚇ⰑⰑⰑⰑ ⰑeⰑⰑ.	It was he that could carry a load furthest.

ᴠ' ᴀıп ᴠᴀ ᵹıoᴘᴀ ᴀ ᵯᴀıᴌᴌ ᵯíᴌe ᵴᴌíᵹe ᴠo ċᴜᴘ ᴠé.	It was on him that it was a very short delay to traverse a mile of space.
ᴠᴀ ᴠeᴀᵴ é!	It was a nice thing!
ᴠᴀ ᵯᴀıᴄ é!	It was a good thing!
ᴠᴀ ᴠᴘeᴀᵹ é!	It was a fine thing!
ᴠᴀ ᵯóᴘ é	It was a big thing!
ᴅoᴠ oᴌc é!	It was a bad thing!
ᴠᴀ ᴄᴘéᴀn é!	It was a brave thing!
ᴠᴀ ċᴘᴜínn é!	It was an exact thing!
ᴅoᴠ ᵱíoᴘ é!	It was a true thing!
ᴅoᴠ í ᴀn ᵱíᴘınne í.	It was the truth.
ᴠí ᴠᴘıᴀn 'nᴀ ᴘíᵹ.	Brian was king.
ᴠí ᵴé 'nᴀ ᴘíᵹ ᴜᴀᴘᴀᴌ.	He was a noble king.
ᴠí ᵴé cóᵯᴀċᴛᴀċ.	He was powerful.
ᴠí ᵴé ı n' ᵱeᴀᴘ ᵯᴀıᴄ.	He was a good man.
ᴠí ᵴé ı n' ᵱeᴀᴘ ᵱóᵹᴀnᴛᴀ.	He was a useful man.
ᴠí ᴀn ᴌá ᵹo h-ᴀoíᴠınn.	The day was splendid.
ᴠí ᴀn ᴌá ᵹo h-ᴀnᴀ ᴀoíᴠınn.	The day was most splendid
ᴠí ᴀn ᴌá ᴄıᴘm.	The day was dry.
ᴠí ᴀn ᴌá ᴀnᴀ ᴠᴘoᴄᴀᴌᴀċ.	The day was very hot.
ᴠí ᴀn ᵱeᴀᴘ ᴌáıᴅıᴘ.	The man was strong.
ᴠí ᵴé ᴀnᴀ ᴌáıᴅıᴘ.	He was very strong.
ᴠí ᵴé ᴌᴀᵹ.	He was weak.
ᴠí ᵴé ᴀnᴀ ᴌᴀᵹ.	He was very weak.
ᴠí ᵴé ᵹo ᴌᴀᵹ.	He was weakly.
ᴠí ᵴé ᵹo h-ᴀnᴀ ᴌᴀᵹ.	He was in a very weak state.
ᴠí ᵴé ᵹo h-ᴀnᴀ ᴌᴀᵹ ᴀᴘ ᵱᴀᴅ.	He was in a very weak state entirely.

bí ré ʒo ꝺeaʃ.	He was nice. He was very nicely off.
bí ré ʒo h-ana ꝺeaʃ.	He was very nice. He was very nicely off.
bíoꝺ ré aʒ ól.	He used to drink.
bíoꝺ ré aʃ meiʃʒe.	He used to be drunk.
bíoꝺ ré aʒ bʃuiʒean.	He used to be fighting.
bíoꝺ ré aʒ acʃan.	He used to be quarrelling.
bíoꝺ caʃc aiʃ.	He used to be thirsty.
bíoꝺ coꝺla aiʃ.	He used to be sleepy.
bíoꝺ canncaʃ aiʃ.	He used to be vexed.
bíoꝺ ocʃaʃ aiʃ.	He used to be hungry.
bíoꝺ bʃuiꝺ aiʃ.	He used to be in a hurry.
bíoꝺ ꝺocáll aiʃ.	He used to be stingy.
bíoꝺ éaꝺ aiʃ.	He used to be jealous.
bíoꝺ ꝺicineaʃ aiʃ.	He used to be in haste.
bíoꝺ leiʃʒe aiʃ.	He used to be lazy.
bíoꝺ buile aiʃ.	He used to be mad.
bíoꝺ ré ʃcólca.	He used to be scalded.
bíoꝺ ré aʃ buile.	He used to be mad.
bíoꝺ ré aʃ ꝺeaʃʒ-buile.	He used to be stark mad.
bíoꝺ ré aʃ a ṁeaḃaiʃ.	He used to be out of his mind.
Iʃ aʃ meiʃʒe a bíoꝺ ré.	It is drunk he used to be.
Iʃ aʒ ól a bíoꝺ ré.	It is drinking he used to be.
Iʃ 'na coꝺla a bí ré.	It is asleep he was.
Iʃ 'na ꝺúiʃeacc acá ré.	It is awake he is.
Iʃ 'na ꝺúiʃeacc a bí ré.	It is awake he was.
Iʃ 'na coꝺla a bíoꝺ ré nuaiʃ bíꝺinn-ʃe am ꝺúiʃeacc.	It is asleep he used to be when I used to be awake.

Ifé an coola if feáf leif.	It is (the) sleep he likes best.
U' é an coola oob feáf leif.	What he liked best was the sleep.
Ifé an coola oob feáf leif.	Sleep *is* the thing he *liked* best.

In the last eight phrases " if " *is the statement of a* GENERAL TRUTH, *and suits all times,* PAST, PRESENT *and* FUTURE. *In such sentences it is usually omitted,* e.g. :—

Af meifge atá fé.	[It is] drunk he is.
Ag ól a bíoo fé.	[It is] drinking he used to be.
'Na coola a beió fé.	[It is] asleep he will be.

Sometimes it is introduced into the middle of the sentence in the form of " ifeao," e.g. :—

Af meifge ifeao atá fé.	Drunk is what he is.
Ag ól ifeao a bíon fé.	Drinking is what he does be at.
'Na coola ifeao a beió fé.	Asleep is what he will be.
Ag fiúbal ifeao atá fé.	[It is] walking he is.
Ag funt atá fé.	[It is] running he is.
If agamfa atá fé. Agamfa ifeao atá fé. Agamfa atá fé.	}It is I that have it.
If feaf é fin. Feaf ifeao é fin. Feaf é fin.	}*That* is a man.
Ifé an lá amáfac an Domnac. Amáfac an Domnac.	}To-morrow is Sunday. (Lit., It is to-morrow th ; Sunday is.)

Ир ᴅⱶine é.
ᴅⱶine irᴇⱥᴅ é. — It is a human being.
ᴅⱶine ⱥⲧⱥ ⱥnn.

Ⰱⱥ ᴅⱶine é.
ᴅⱶine ᴅoⰱ eⱥᴅ é. — It was a human being.
ᴅⱶine ⱥ ⰱí ⱥnn.

Ир inᴅé ⱥ ⰱíor i ᵹCoрcⱥiᵹ. — It is yesterday I was in
Inᴅé ⱥ ⰱíor i ᵹCoрcⱥiᵹ. — Cork.

Ир inᴅⱶ ⱥⲧⱥim ⱥᵹ ⲧeⱥⲥⲧ ⱥⰱⱥile. — It is to-day I am coming
Inᴅⱶ ⱥⲧⱥim ⱥᵹ ⲧeⱥⲥⲧ ⱥⰱⱥile. — home.

Ир ⱥmⱥрⱥⲥ ⱥ ⲥⱥррⱥᴅ.
ⱥmⱥрⱥⲥ ⱥ ⲥⱥррⱥᴅ. — It is on to-morrow I shall
ⱥmⱥрⱥⲥ irᴇⱥᴅ ⱥ ⲥⱥррⱥᴅ. — return.

Sometimes the very nature of the statement will not allow "ir" to be used in past time.

Ир lⱥiᴅir ⱥⲧⱥ ᴅiⱥрmⱶᴅ. — Dermod is strong.
Ир lⱥiᴅir ⱥ ⰱí ᴅiⱥрmⱶᴅ inᴅé. — Dermod was strong yesterday.
Ир lⱥiᴅir ⱥ ⰱeiᴅ ré ⱥmⱥрⱥⲥ. — He will be strong to-morrow.

But we cannot say :—

Ир lⱥiᴅir ⱥn feⱥr ᴅiⱥрmⱶᴅ nⱶⱥir ⰱí ré óᵹ. *We must say,* ⰱⱥ lⱥiᴅir ⱥn feⱥr ᴅiⱥрmⱶᴅ nⱶⱥir ⱥ ⰱí ré óᵹ, Dermod *was* a strong man when he *was* young. *It does not follow that he is a strong man now. But we can say,* Ир lⱥiᴅir ⱥ ⰱí ᴅiⱥрmⱶᴅ nⱶⱥir ⱥ ⰱí ré óᵹ, *because it* IS *true now that he* WAS *strong then.*

Conditional Sentences,

Má 'r maiṫ é ir miṫiḋ é.	If it is good it is full time for it.
Má 'r cailín ó'n ḋtuaṫ mé ní íorfainn geir.	Even if I am a country girl I would not eat tallow.
Má 'r féidir é tiocfaiḋ Diarmuid.	Dermod will come if it is possible.
Dá mb' féidir é do ṫiocfaḋ ré.	He would have come if it had been possible.
Má tá ciall agat éirtfir.	If you have sense you will keep silent.
Dá mbeiḋeaḋ ciall agat d'éirtfá.	If you had sense you would keep silent.
Má ḃíon ciall aige éirtfiḋ ré.	If he will have sense he will keep silent, or if he has sense he will keep silent.
Ba ṁaiṫ liom deoċ d' fáġail.	I should like to get a drink.
Ba feóiġ an fear Taḋg dá mbeiḋeaḋ airgead aige.	Thade would be a wonderful man if he had money.
Dá mba ṁaiṫ leir é do ḃeiḋeaḋ airgead aige.	He would have money if he liked.
Dá mba ná rgaoilfaḋ ré uaiḋ é ḃeiḋeaḋ ré aige go tiuġ.	If he had not let it go he would have it in abundance.
Má b' fada é an lá ba ġairid í an oiḋce.	If the day was long the night was short.

Ⅾá mb' ꝼá́ⱺá é ᴀn lá ꝺeⅈⱺeáⱺ ᴀn oíⱺċe ᵹᴀⅈꝶⱺ.	If the day had been long the night would have been short.

The difference between ⱺá mbᴀ *and* má bᴀ *is this—* má bᴀ *takes the condition for granted as* REALISED, ⱺá mbᴀ *takes the* OPPOSITE *for granted.*

Má 'ꝛ ⱺuⅈne uᴀꝛᴀl é.	If he is a gentleman (*which I should think he is*), &c.
Ⅾá mbᴀ ⱺuⅈne uᴀꝛᴀl é.	If he were a gentleman (*which he cannot be*), &c.
Má bᴀ ⱺuⅈne uᴀꝛᴀl é.	If he was a gentleman (*as you say he was*), &c.
Má cá ⱺeoċ ᴀᵹᴀm ólꝼᴀⱺ é.	If I have a drink I shall drink it.
Ⅾá mbeⅈⱺeᴀⱺ ⱺeoċ ᴀᵹᴀm ⱺ' ólꝼᴀⅈnn é.	If I had a drink I would drink it.
Má cá ꝛé ᴀᵹᴀm ᵹeᴀbᴀⅈꝛé.	If I have it you will get it.
Ⅾá mbeⅈⱺeᴀⱺ ꝛé ᴀᵹᴀm ᵹeᴀbcá é.	If I had it you would get it.
Má 'ꝛ ᴀᵹᴀmꝛᴀ ᴀcá ꝛé ᵹeᴀbᴀⅈꝛ é.	If *I* have it you will get it.
Ⅾá mb' ᴀᵹᴀmꝛᴀ beⅈⱺeᴀⱺ ꝛé ᵹeᴀbcá é.	If *I* had it you would get it.
Má 'ꝛ ᴀᵹ ⅈmceᴀċc ᴀcá ꝛé ⱺeᴀꝛꝼᴀⱺ leⅈꝛ ꝼᴀnṁᴀⅈnc.	If it is going he is, I shall bid him stay.
Ⅾá mb' ᴀᵹ ⅈmceᴀċc ᴀ beⅈⱺeᴀⱺ ꝛé ⱺeᴀꝛꝼᴀⅈnn leⅈꝛ ꝼᴀnṁᴀⅈnc.	If he was going I would bid him stay.

Má 'r ocṗaṗ aṫá aiṗ taḃ-aṗṗaḃ ṗuḃ le n-iṫeaḃ ḋó.	If it is hungry he is, I shall give him something to eat.
Ḋá mb' ocṗaṗ a ḃeiḃeaḃ aiṗ taḃaṗṗainn ṗuḃ le n-iṫeaḃ ḋó.	If he was hungry I would give him something to eat.
Má 'r ḋóṁṗa a ṫuṡaiṗ é tá ṗé aṡam.	If it is to me you gave it, I have it.
Ḋá mba ḋóṁṗa taḃaṗṗá é ḃeiḃeaḃ ṗé aṡam.	If you had given it to me I should have it.
Má 'r 'na coḋla aṫá ṗé ní 'l baoṡal aiṗ.	If it is asleep he is, he is all right.
Ḋá mba' na coḋla ḃeiḃ-eaḃ ṗé ní ḃeiḃeaṫ bao-ṡal aiṗ.	If he were asleep he would be all right; there would be no danger of him.
Má tá a tuilleaḃ aṡam ṡeaḃaiṗ é.	If I have any more you'll get it.
Ḋá mbeiḃeaḃ a tuilleaḃ aṡam ṡeaḃtá é.	If I had any more you should get it.
Ba ṁait liom ḋá ḃṗéaḋ-ainn ṗaḃaṗc ḋ' ṗaṡail aiṗ.	I should like if I could get a view of it.
Ba ṁait liom ṡo laḃaṗṗá.	I should like you to speak.
Ba ṁait liom ṡo n-éiṗtṗá.	I should like you to keep silent.
Ba ṁait liom ṡo ḋtiocṗá aṡur laḃaiṗt liom.	I should like you to come and speak to me.
Ba ṁait liom ṡo ḃṗanṗá toiṗ ṗa ḃaile ḋuit ṗéin.	I should like you to remain east at home for yourself.
Ḋá mb' áil leat éiṗteaċt ḃeiḋinn ana ḃuiḃeaċ ḋíot.	If you would hold your tongue I would be very much obliged to you.

Dob feárr de tu é dá mbá ná beiðeað a leát oipeað cainte agat.	You would be the better of it if you had not one half the talk.
Dá mbá ná beiðeað tart aip ní ólfað sé.	If he were not thirsty he would not drink.
Muna mbeiðeað go bfuil tart aip ní ólfað sé.	But that he is thirsty he would not drink.
Muna mbeiðeað tart do ðeit aip ní ólfað sé.	But for his being thirsty he would not drink.
Muna mbeiðeað tart aip ní ólfað sé.	If he were not thirsty he would not drink.
Muna raib tart aip níor ól sé.	If he was not thirsty he did not drink.
Muna mbeiðeað go raib tart aip ní ólfað sé.	But that he was thirsty he would not drink.
Muna bfuil tart aip ní ólfað sé.	If he is not thirsty he will not drink.

The learner must note carefully the difference between those seven forms of a negative condition, especially between muna raib *and* muna mbeiðeað go raib, *as well as between* muna bfuil *and* muna mbeiðeað go bfuil. Muna bfuil *means* If there is not. Muna mbeiðeað go bfuil *means* But for the fact that there is. Muna raib *means* If there was not. Muna mbeiðeað go raib *means* But for the fact that there was.

Má 'r rud é go bfanfaip go lá tar go teine.	If it is a thing that you will stay till morning come as far as the fire.

Dá mba puð é go bfanfá go lá níop mirðe ðuit teact go dtí an teine.	If it was a thing that you would stay till morning you might come to the fire.
Dá mba puð é go dtiocfá ap fanṁaint go lá níop mór ðuit rgéala ðo cup aðaile.	If it was a thing that you would come on staying until morning you would want to send word home.
Ap iapaip aip, má ba puð é go bfaifað ré go lá, rgéala ðo cup aðaile?	Did you ask him to send word home if it was a thing that he would stay till morning?

In this sentence, má ba puð é *intimates the speaker's approval.* Dá mba puð é *would intimate the speaker's indifference, or disapproval, of the party's remaining.*

Dá mba puð é go bfaṡainn fiće púnt ap an gcapalagurðeić púint ap an mboin ir beag ná go mbeiðeað an leatćíor agam.	If it was a thing that I would get twenty pounds for the horse and ten pounds for the cow, I would have nearly the half-year's-rent.
Dá mba puð é go mbeiðeað an lá amápać ap fóṡnaṁ ð' feaðraiðe cruać ðo ðéanaṁ ðe 'n feup rain tíor.	If it was a thing that to-morrow would be any way fair, a rick could be made of that hay below.
Dúbapt leir má ba puð é go mbeiðeað an lá ap fóṡnaṁ, cruać ðo ðéanaṁ ðe 'n feup.	I told him, if the day was any way fair, to make a rick of the hay.

Here, má ba puo é *intimates that the day* DID *turn out fine.* Oá mba puo é *would intimate that it* DID NOT.

Munapuo é ʒo oꞇaiꞇnꞃió an áiꞇ leaꞇ ꞃéaoꞃaiꞃ imꞇeaꞇ aꞃ.	If it is not a thing that you will like the place you can leave it.
Oúbaiꞃꞇ leiꞃ oá mba puo é ná ꞇaiꞇnꞃaó an áiꞇ leiꞃ ná ꞃaib bac aiꞃ imꞇeaꞇ aꞃ.	I told him that if he happened not to like the place he was at liberty to leave it.
Má 'ꞃ puo é ʒo mbeió an bliaʒain ꞃeo cóm maiꞇ leiꞃ an mbliaʒain anaipiʒ beió an ꞃaoʒal ꞃuaꞃ.	If it turns out that this year will be as good as last year was, the times will be at the height of prosperity.
Oá mba puo é ʒo mbeióeaó an bliaʒain ꞃeo cóm maiꞇ aʒuꞃ bí an bliaʒain anaipiʒ beiómíꞃ aꞃ áꞃ oꞇoil.	If this year had turned out as good as last year we would be as well off as we could wish.

"iꞃ" relative.

An ꞇ-é iꞃ ꞃíʒ.	The man who is king.
"An ꞃúmaiꞃe iꞃ aꞇaiꞃ ouiꞇ."	"That mope who is father to you."
An ꞇ-é iꞃ ꞃeaꞃ ꞇíʒe anꞃo.	The person who is man-of-the-house here.
Cia h-é iꞃ ceann anꞃo?	Who is boss here?
Cia h-é iꞃ ʒiolla aʒaib?	Who is your guide?
Cia h-é iꞃ ꞃeaꞃ cínn ꞃiain oꞃaib?	Who is your leader?

Δn τ-é ιτ ʒιοℓℓλ λʒαιnn | The person who is our
ιτέ ιτ ϝελτ cînn τιλιn | guide it is he who is our
οτλιnn. | leader.
Δn τ-é ιτ ϝλʋλ cοτ ιτέ ιτ | The man who is long of
ϝλʋλ τιυτℓόʒ. | leg it is he who is long
 | of step.

In this Irish construction cοτ *and* τιυτℓόʒ *express*
MANNER, *exactly as* " of leg " *and* " of step " *do in the
English.* Τιυτℓόʒ *is the step which is taken when a
person springs off one leg and alights on the other.*

Δn τ-é ιτ móτ cλιnτ ní | Often the person who is
τι-é ιτ μλιτ cιλℓℓ ʒο | great of speech is not
μιniτ. | the person who is good
 | in sense.

Iτ μιniτ nλċ é λn τ-é ιτ | It often happens that it
υλτλℓ cáιℓ ιτ υλτλℓ | is not the person who
méιnn. | enjoys the noble name
 | that has the noble dis-
 | position.

The ιτ *which grammarians set down as the* SIGN *of
the superlative, is in reality nothing but this relative*
ιτ. Δn ϝελτ ιτ móτ cλιnτ *is exactly the same construction as* λn ϝελτ ιτ mó cλιnτ.

Δn ϝελτ ιτ móτ cλιnτ. | The person who has much
 | talk.
Δn ϝελτ ιτ mó cλιnτ | The person who has more
 | talk (*than anyone else*),
 | *i.e.*, the man who has
 | *most* talk.

An feaṙ iṙ feáṙ.	The man who is better (than any one else), *i.e.*, the man who is best.
An feaṙ iṙ óiġe.	The man who is younger (than any one else), *i.e.*, the man who is youngest.
An feaṙ iṙ ṙine.	The man who is older (than any one else), *i.e.*, oldest.
An feaṙ ba ṫṙeiṙe.	T h e m a n w h o *w a s* stronger (than any one else), *i.e.*, the man who *was* strongest.
An feaṙ ṙoob óiġe.	The man who *was* younger (than any one else), *i.e.*, the man who *was* the youngest.
An feaṙ ṙoob feáṙ.	The man who was better (than any one else), *i.e.*, the man who was best.
An feaṙ ba ṁó cainc.	The person who *had* more talk (than any one else), *i.e.*, the man who *had* most talk.
An feaṙ ba ṁóṙ cainc.	The man who *was* of much talk, *i.e.*, the man who had a lot of talk.
Ba ṁinic naṙ ḃ' é an feaṙ ṙoob uaṙal cáil an feaṙ ṙoob uaṙal méinn.	It frequently happened that it was not the person who had the high name that had the noble disposition.

Cáil *and* méinn *are substantives of* MANNER.

An c-é ꝺob ꝼaꝺa coꞃ b' é ꝺob ꝼaꝺa cꞃuꞃlóg.	The person who had the long leg was the person who had the long step.
An c-é ba ꞡiolla aꞡainn iꞃé b' ꝼeaꞃ cinn ꞃiain oꞃainn.	The person who was our guide is the person who was our leader.

In old Irish this relative iꞃ *was often written* aꞃ, *as if compounded of* a *and* iꞃ; *e.g.,* "Ꝺobeꞃcaꞃ ꝺuic-ꞃiu ꞃin" ol Cacal "ocuꞃ ni cuꞡaꝺ ꞃeimpi ná ina ꝺiaiꝺ co bꞃuinꝺe bꞃáca ní aꞃ leꞃciu linn olcáꞃ ꞃin." "That shall be granted to thee," said Cathal, "and there has not been given before it, nor after it until the brink of judgment, a thing *which is* more disagreeable to us than that." (See Aiꞃlinꞡe Meic Conꞡlinne, page 59.)

The relative form of cá *is* acá. Acá *should never be used as an absolute form.*

Cá ꞃé 'na coꝺla.	He is asleep.
'Na coꝺla acá ꞃé.	It is asleep he is.
'Na coꝺla acá ꞃí.	It is asleep she is.
Ꝼáꞡ maꞃ acá ꞃé é.	Leave him as he is.
"An c-é acá ꞃuaꞃ ólcaꞃ ꝺeoc aiꞃ."	"The man who is prosperous people drink his health."
"An c-é acá ꞃioꞃ buailceaꞃ coꞃ aiꞃ."	"The man who is down people trample on him."
Cáim ꞡo maic.	I am very well.

Ḟáᵹ maṟ atáim mé.	Leave me as I am.
Ᵹo ṟó ṁaiṫ atáim.	It is right well I am.
Iṟ ᵹo h-ana ṁaiṫ atáim.	It is mighty well I am.
Ᵹo ꝺian ṁaiṫ iṟeaꝺ atáim.	Exceedingly well is what I am.
Táim ᵹo h-ana ṁaiṫ.	I am mighty well.
Táim ᵹo ꝺian ṁaiṫ.	I am exceedingly well.
" Ꝺaṟ ꝼiaꝺ táimṟe aṟ meiṟᵹe ! "	" Really, *I* am drunk."
Ḃí Seaᵹan ua Manᵹáin ann.	John Mangan was there.
Iṟé Seaᵹan ua Manᵹáin a ḃí ann.	It is John Mangan that was there.
Ḃí bean Ṡeaᵹain ui Manᵹáin ann.	John Mangan's wife was there.
Ḃean Ṡeaᵹáin ui Manᵹáin a ḃí ann.	It was John Mangan's wife that was there.
Ḃí an ṟᵹéal maṟ ṟin.	The matter stood in that way.
Sin maṟ a ḃí an ṟᵹéal.	That is how the matter stood.
Maṟ a ḃí ṟé.	As it was.
Maṟ atá ṟé.	As it is.
'Maṟ a ḃeiꝺ ṟé.	As it will be.
Maṟ a ḃíoꝺ ṟé.	As it used to be.
Maṟ a ḃeiꝺeaꝺ ṟé.	As it would be.
Ḃí ṟé maṟ atá ṟé.	It was as it is.
Tá ṟé maṟ a ḃeiꝺ ṟé.	It is as it will be.
Ḃeiꝺ ṟé maṟ a ḃíoꝺ ṟé.	It will be as it used to be.
Ḃíoꝺ ṟé maṟ a ḃíon ṟé.	It used to be as it does be.

bíon ré maṟ a bíoḃ ré.	It does be as it used to be.
Iṟ aʒ ceaċc acá Domnall.	It is coming Donald is.
Cá Dómnall aʒ ceaċc.	Donald is coming.
An c-é acá 'na ʒiolla aʒainn iṟé acá i n' ḟeaṟ cínn ṟiain aʒainn.	The person whom we have as guide is the person whom we have as leader

In dependent sentences iṟ *becomes* ʒuṟ *or* ʒuṟaḃ.

Deiṟim ʒuṟ ḃeáʒ an lá é.	I say that it is a *fine* day.
Deiṟim ʒuṟ lá ḃeáʒ é.	I say that it is a fine day.
Deiṟim ʒuṟaḃ áluinn an lá é.	I say that it is a glorious day.
Meaṟaim ʒuṟ ḟeaṟ láiḋiṟ é.	I consider that he is a strong man.
Ceapaim ʒuṟ anṟo acá ṟé.	I conclude that it is here it is
Iṟ dóiċ liom ʒuṟ cṟeiṟe ḋ' ḟeaṟ Caḋʒ 'ná Domnall.	I think that Thade is a stronger *man* than Donald.
Cṟeiḋim ʒuṟ ḟeaṟcainn a ḋeanḟaiḋ ṟé.	I believe it is rain that will come.
Ní deiṟim 'ná ʒuṟ aʒ ṟioc acá ṟé.	I don't say but that it is freezing it is.
Ní deiṟim 'ná ʒo ḃḟuil an ceaṟc aʒac.	I don't say but you are right.
Ní deiṟim 'ná ʒuṟ aʒac acá an ceaṟc.	I don't say but that it is you that's right.

c

Dúḃaꞃꞇ ꞡuꞃ ḃꞃeáꞡ an lá é.	I said that it was a fine day.
Dúḃaꞃꞇ ꞡuꞃ lá ḃꞃeáꞡ é.	I said that it was a fine day.
Dúḃaꞃꞇ ꞅé ꞡuꞃ ᵭꞃoċ lá é.	He said that it was a bad day.
Dúḃaꞃꞇ ꞅé ꞡuꞃ ḃ' áluinn an lá é.	He said that it was a glorious day.
Meaꞅaꞃ ꞡuꞃ ḃ' ꞓeaꞃ láꞁ-ᵭiꞃ é.	I thought that he was a strong man.
Ceapaꞃ ꞡuꞃ anꞅo a ḃí ꞅé.	I thought that it was here he was.
Má ᵭeiꞃim ꞡuꞃ ḃꞃeáꞡ an lá é ᵭéaꞃꝼaᵭ an ꝼiꞃinne.	If I say that it is a fine day I shall say the truth.
Má ᵭeiꞃim ꞡuꞃ ḃꞃeáꞡ an lá é ᵭeiꞃim an ꝼiꞃinne.	If I say that it is a fine day I say the truth.
Dá n-aḃꞃainn ꞡuꞃ ḃꞃeáꞡ an lá é ᵭéaꞃꝼainn an ꝼiꞃinne.	If I were to say that it is a fine day I would say the truth.
Dá n-aḃꞃainn ꞡuꞃ ḃꞃeáꞡ an lá é ᵭéaꞃꝼainn an ꝼiꞃinne.	If I were to say that it was a fine day I would say the truth.

In dependent sentences ní *becomes* ná, náċ, *and* níoꞃ *becomes* náꞃ *or* náꞃ ḃ'.

Ní h-olc an lá é.	It is not a bad day.
Deiꞃim náċ olc an lá é.	I say that it is not a bad day.
Níoꞃ ḃ' olc an lá é.	It was not a bad day.

Oúbaɾc náɾ b' olc an lá é.	I said that it was not a bad day.
Níoɾ caillead é.	I did not lose it.
Oúbaɾc náɾ caillead é.	I said that I did not lose it.
Ní h-admad cloc.	Stone is not wood.
Oeiɾim nác admad cloc.	I say that stone is not wood.
Oúbaɾc náɾ b' admad cloc.	I said that stone was not wood.
Ní ɣadaɾ coinín.	A rabbit is not a dog.
Oeiɾim nác ɣadaɾ coinín.	I say that a rabbit is not a dog.
Oúbaɾc náɾ ɣadaɾ coinín.	I said that a rabbit was not a dog.
Má deiɾ duine ɣuɾ ɣadaɾ cóinín ní deiɾ ɾé an fíɾinne.	If a person says that a rabbit is a dog he does not say the truth.
Oá n-abɾad duine ɣuɾ ɣadaɾ an coinín ní déaɾɾad ɾé an fíɾinne.	If a person were to say that the rabbit is a dog he would not say the truth.
Má abɾan duine ɣuɾ ɣadaɾ coinín ní déaɾɾad ɾé an fíɾinne.	If a person say that a rabbit is a dog he will not say the truth.
Oúbaɾcɾa, dá n-abɾad duine ɣuɾ ɣadaɾ coinín, ná déaɾɾad ɾé an fíɾinne.	I said, that if a person were to say that a rabbit was a dog, he would not say the truth.
Oúbaɾc Oómnall ɣo ndúbaɾcɾa, dá n-abɾad duine ɣuɾ cóinín	Donald said that *I* said that if a person were to say that a dog was a

ʓaḃaṇ ná ṽéaṇḟaṽ ṇé an ḟíṇinne.

rabbit he would not say the truth.

Ʒuṇ a' maiṫ aʒaṫ!

Thank you!

Náṇ a' maiṫ aʒaṫ!

No thanks to you!

Ʒuṇ a' míle maiṫ aʒaṫ!

Thank you ever so much!

Náṇ a' míle maiṫ aʒaṫ!

In downright defiance of you!

Ʒuṇ a' ṇeaċṫ ḟeáṇ a ḃeiṽ-miṽ ḃliaʒan ó 'ṇṽiu aʒuṛ muna ḟeáṇ náṇ a' meaṛa!

That we may be seven times better off this day twelve months, and if we are not better that we may not be worse!

Ṫá Ṫaṽʒ ṫaṇ éiṛ ḃáiṛ, ʒuṇ a' maiṫ an ṁaiṛe ṽó é!

Thade has died, may he have fared well by it!

Ṫá ṛé aṇ ṛliʒ na ḟíṇinne, ʒuṇ a' maiṫ an ṁaiṛe ṽó é!

He is gone to the other world, may he be happy in the matter!

Ṫá ṛʒéala maiṫe aʒam ṽuiṫ. Ʒuṇ a' ṛláṇ ṛʒéalaiṽe!

I have good tidings for you. Health to the bringer of the tidings!

Ʒuṇ a' ḟeáṇ amáṇaċ ṫu!

May you be better to-morrow!

Ṫá áṫaṛ oṛm.

I am glad.

Ḃion áṫaṛ oṛm.

I do be glad.

Ḃí áṫaṛ oṛm.

I was glad.

Ḃíoṽ áṫaṛ oṛm.

I used to be glad.

Ḃeiṽ áṫaṛ oṛm.

I shall be glad.

Ḃeiṽeaṽ áṫaṛ oṛm.

I would be glad.

Ḃ' ḟéiṽiṇ ʒo mḃeiṽeaṽ áṫaṛ oṛm.

Perhaps I would be glad.

biou átar opm.	Let me be glad.
Má tá átar opm.	If I am glad.
Dá mbeideað átar opm.	If I were glad.
Ba maiṫ liom átar do beiṫ opm.	I should like to be glad.
If maiṫ liom átar do beiṫ opm.	I like to be glad.
Ní maiṫ liom gan átar do beiṫ opm.	I do not like not to be glad.
Níop maiṫ liom gan átar do beiṫ opm.	I should not like not to be glad.
Tátap ċugat.	(They) are going to be at you.
Tátap ao leanṁaint.	(They) are following you.
Tátap ag feiteaṁ leat.	(They) are waiting for you.
Tátap ag faipe opt.	(They) are watching you.
Tátap ap do ṫí.	(They) are bent on injuring you.
Conup atátap agaib ?	How goes it with ye ?
Tátap maiṫ go leóp.	It goes pretty well.
Bíoteap ag piúbal ap an gcopán po.	(People) do be walking on this path.
Bíoteap am leanṁaint.	(They) do be following me.
Bíoteap ag caint ann.	(Some one) does be talking there.
Bíoteap ag glaoðaċ opm.	(Some one) does be calling me.
Bíoteap ag magað fúm.	(The people) do be making game of me.
Bíoteap ag guið apbaip uaim.	(Some one) does be stealing my corn.

Bíóceaṗ ag caiteaṁ na gcloċ liom.	(They) do be throwing the stones at me.
Bíóceaṗ ag maṗḃaó na gceanc oṗm.	(They) do be killing my hens.
Do ḃíóceaṗ ag glaoóaċ oṗm.	(Some one) was calling me.
Bíóceaṗ ag faiṗe oṗm.	(Some one) was watching me.
Bíóceaṗ ag ṗiúḃal am óiaió.	There was (some one) walking after me.
Bíóceaṗ ṗóṁam aṗ an mḃóċaṗ.	(The party) was before me on the road.
Bíóci ag glaoóaċ oṗm.	(Some one) used to be calling me.
Bíóci ag faiṗe oṗm.	(Some one) used to be watching me.
Bíóci ag caiteaṁ na gcloċ liom.	(Some one) used to be throwing the stones at me.
Beióṗaṗ ċugac.	(They) will be at you.
Beióṗaṗ ag ceaċc.	(Some one) will be coming.
Beióṗaṗ ag imceaċc a-máṗaċ.	(They) will be leaving on to-morrow.
An mbeióṗaṗ ag gaḃáil o' féuṗ inoiu ?	Shall (we) be at hay to-day.
An mbeióṗaṗ ollaṁ ċuige ?	Shall (we) be ready for it ?
Beióṗaṗ.	Yes, (we) shall.
Má ċáċaṗ ollaṁ inoiu beióṗaṗ ollaṁ amáṗaċ.	If (we) are ready to-day we shall be ready to-morrow.

Dá mbeiḋfí ollaṁ inḋiu ḋo ḃeiḋfí ollaṁ a-máṙac.

If (we) were ready to-day (we) would be ready to-morrow.

Má ḃíḋteaṙ ollaṁ a-noċt beiḋfaṙ ollaṁ amáṙac.

If (we) are ready to-night (we) shall be ready to-morrow.

An ḃfuilteaṙ ollaṁ?

Are (people) ready?

An mbíḋteaṙ ollaṁ?

Do (they) be ready?

An mbíḋteaṙ aṡ ṡlaoḋaċ oṙt?

Does (any person) be calling you?

An mbíḋteaṙ aṡ caiteaṁ cloċ leat?

Does (any person) be throwing stones at you?

Bíḋteaṙ.

Yes.

Deiṙim ṡo mbíḋteaṙ.

I say there does.

Dúḃaṙt ṡo mbíḋtí.

I said there used to be.

An ṙaḃtaṙ aṡ ṡlaoḋaċ oṙt inḋiu?

Was there (anyone) call-ing you to-day?

Ní ṙaḃtaṙ.

There was not.

An ḃfuilteaṙ aṡ ṡlaoḋaċ oṙt anoiṙ?

Is there (anyone) calling you now?

Ní fuilteaṙ. Ní 'lteaṙ

There is not.

An ḃfuilteaṙ ċúṡam?

Is (anyone) going to be at me?

Táṫaṙ.

Yes there is (some one).

Bíḋteaṙ aṡ faiṙe aiṙ.

Let (some one) be watch-ing him.

Bí aḋ ṙuiġe!

Get up at once!

Bí meaṙ!

Be quick!

Bí amuiċ!

Go out at once!

Bí aṙ ṙiúḃal!

Go away!

Bí aṡ ṡluaiṙeaċt!

Be moving!

Bí ag imṫeaċt!	Be going!
Ná bí ad ṡeasaṁ ansain!	Don't remain standing there!
Coruig agus ná bíḋtear ag feiṫeaṁ leat!	Make haste lest (the people) may be waiting for you!
Ná bí am ḃoḋraḋ!	Don't be bothering me!
Ná bí ag magaḋ fúṫ féin!	Don't be making game of yourself, *i.e.*, don't be making a fool of yourself.
Ná bí ag leigint na gaoiṫe isteaċ.	Don't be letting the wind in, *i.e.*, don't be talking absurdly.
Conus 'taoi?	How are you?
An ḃfuil 'n tu go diaḃulta?	Are you exceedingly well?

Some of our Irish scholars are under an extraordinary misapprehension regarding this word diaḃulta. *They imagine it is derived from the word* diaḃal = devil. *It is not. It simply means* "*redoubled.*" *When some of our learned men meet* diaḃulta *they call it* "like a fiend." *But when they meet* cóicdiabulta, *they have to call it what it really means,* "five-fold."

The people's instinct has enabled them to give the true meaning of the word in their own broken English. Here is how they manage it:—

Tá sé ag sioc.	"It is freezing."
Tá sé ag sioc go diaḃulta.	"It is freezing GREATLY."

Tá ré ag feaptainn.	"It is raining."
Tá ré ag feaptainn go diabulta.	"It is raining GREATLY."
Tá Taóg ag puit.	"Thade is running."
Tá ré ag puit go diabulta.	"He is running GREATLY."
Tá ré ag riúbal go diabulta.	"He is walking GREATLY."
Tá ré ag fár go diabulta.	"He is growing GREATLY."
Tá ré ag obair go diabulta.	"He is working GREATLY."
An bfuil an coirce go mait agaib ?	"Have ye the oats good?"
Ac! Tá ré go diabulta againn.	"Ach! We have it GREATLY."
Táid na prátaíde go diabulta ar fad againn.	"We have the potatoes GREAT ENTIRELY."

The word *diabulta* expresses intensity. It is like the word REDOUBLED in English, both as to origin and meaning. There is a word which is derived from *diabal* = devil. It is the word *diabail*. The people invariably translate it "divilish."

Ir diabail an obair í.	"It is devilish work."
Ir diabalta an obair í.	"It is AWFUL work."
Ir diabalta an duine é le feabar.	"He is an awfully good man."
Ir diabalta an duine é le cruinnear.	"He is an awfully exact man."

42

Iʃ ᴅiaḃalᴄa an capal é
ċum oiḃʃe.

"He is a GREAT horse for
work."

Iʃ ᴅiaḃalᴄa an ᴄalaṁ é
ċum óʃnan.

"It is GREAT land for
barley."

Iʃ ᴅiaḃalᴄa an ʃᵹeal é
ná ʃanʃá ʃocaiʃ.

"It is an extraordinary
thing that you would
not keep quiet."

Naċ ᴅiaḃalᴄa ná leiᵹʃaᴅ
ʃiḃ ᴅom ʃéin !

"Is it not extraordinary
that ye would not let
me alone !"

Naċ ᴅiaḃalᴄa ná leiᵹʃaᴅ
ʃiḃ ᴅom ʃéin!

"Is it not extraordinary
that ye would let *my-
self* alone !

Leiᵹ ᴅom ʃéin.

Let me alone.

Leiᵹ ᴅom ʃéin.

Let myself alone.

Ná ḃac é ʃéin.

Don't mind it.

Ná ḃac é ʃéin !

Don't mind itself.

Naċ ᴅiaḃalᴄa an ᴅiċ-
neaʃ aᴄá oʃᴄ !

What an awful hurry you
are in !

Naċ ᴅiaḃail an ᴅiċneaʃ
aᴄá oʃᴄ !

What a divilish hurry you
are in !

Iʃ ᴅiaḃalᴄa an ʃuinneaṁ
a ḃion le pléuʃ.

A bullet moves with very
great force.

Iʃ ᴅiaḃalᴄa a ḃʃuil ᴅ'
aiʃᵹeaᴅ aᵹ Ᵹaᴅᵹ.

Thade has an awful lot of
money.

Iʃ ᴅiaḃalᴄa a ḃʃuil ᴅe
ċainᴄ aiᵹe pé aiʃᵹeaᴅ
aᴄá aiᵹe.

He has an awful lot of
talk whatever money
he has.

Ní beaᵹ ᴅe ʃeó aḃʃuil
ᴅe ċainᴄ aiᵹe.

(*Lit.* It is not too little
as a wonder what talk
he has.) The amount
of talk he has is amazing.

ní beᵹ ᴅ' ionᵹna é.	(*Lit.* It is not too little as a wonder.) It is a very great wonder.
ní beaᵹ liom ᴅé.	I have got enough of it.
ní beaᵹ liom ᴅíob.	I have got enough of them.
ní beaᵹ ᴅom péin an méiᴅ peo.	This much is enough for *me.*
ní móp ᴅom péin an méiᴅ peo.	This much is little enough for myself.
ní móp liom ᴅuiᴄ é.	I don't grudge it to you.
ní móp ᴅuiᴄ é.	You want it.
ní beaᵹ ᴅuiᴄ é.	It is enough for you.
ᴄá pé pó móp aᵹaᴄ.	It is too big for you.
ᴄá pé pó beaᵹ aᵹaᴄ.	It is too small for you.
ᴄá pé pó láiᴅip ᴅuiᴄ.	It is too strong for you.
ᴄá pé pó laᵹ ᴅuiᴄ.	It is too weak for you.
ᴄá pé pó laᵹ aᵹaᴄ.	You have it too weak.
ᴄá pé pó ᴄeann aᵹaᴄ.	You have made it too stiff.
ᴄá pé pó boᵹ aᵹaᴄ.	You have it too slack.
ᴄá pé pó boᵹ ᴅuiᴄ.	It is too slack for you.
ᴄá pé cam aᵹaᴄ.	You have bent it.
ᴄá pé ollaṁ aᵹam.	I have prepared it; I have made it ready.
ᴄá pé lán aᵹam.	I have filled it; I have it full.
ᴄá pé pocaip aᵹam.	I have settled it; I have it settled.
ᴄá pé ipᴄiᵹ aᵹam.	I have brought it in; I have it brought in; I have it in: I have it inside

Tá ré amuiċ agam.	I have put it out; I have it put out; I have it out; I have it outside.
Tá ré ar lár agam.	I have thrown it down; I have it thrown down; I have it down; I have it on the ground.
Tá ré tuar agam.	I have put it up; I have it put up; I have it up; I have it above.
Tá ré ruar agam.	(*This is the same as the previous sentence, but it expresses the* upward *motion, not the rest* above. *This distinction cannot be expressed in English.*)
Tá ré tíor agam.	I have taken it down below: I have it carried down; I have it down: I have it below.
Tá ré ríor agam.	(*The same distinction as in the previous case.*)
Tá ré tall agam.	I have taken it over; I have it carried over; I have it over, yonder.
Tá ré anonn agam.	(*The same distinction.*)
Cá ré aḃur agam.	I have brought it here; I have it brought here; I have it here.

Tá ré anall agam.	I have brought it over; I have it brought over; I have it over, here.
Tá an teine ap lapaó agam.	I have lighted the fire; I have the fire lighted; I have the fire lighting.
Tá an t-áptaċ folaṁ agam.	I have emptied the vessel; I have the vessel emptied; I have the vessel empty.
Táió na ba i oteanta 'céile agam.	I have collected the cattle; I have the cattle collected; I have the cattle together.
Ifiaó mo ba féin iaó.	They are my own cows.
Ifiaó iaó.	They are the same.
Ní h-iaó fo iaó !	These are not they !
An iaó fo iaó ?	Are these they?
Ní h-iaó.	They are not.
Tá ouine ag teaċt.	There is a person coming.
An é Oiapmuio é ?	Is it Dermod?
Ní h-é.	It is not.
An é a ṁac é ?	Is it his son?
An bó atá ann ?	Is it a cow?
If bó. ⎫ Ifeaó. ⎭	Yes.
An í an bó atá ann ?	Is it the cow?
Ifí.	Yes.
Biteaṁnaċ ifeaó í. If-eaó fan.	She is a thief, so she is.
Tá ré 'na lá, tá fan.	It is day, so it is.

'Ná lá ireaд aтá ré. Ir-
eaд ran.

Broken is how you have it,
so it is.

Day is what it is, so it is.

Ḃuirтe ireaд aтá ré
aзaт. Ireaд ran.

Broken is how you have it,
so it is.

'Ná rmiдiṗiníḃ aтá ré
aзaт. Ireaд ran.

In smithereens is how you
have it, so it is.

'Ná ḃрúrзaṗ aтá ré aзaт.
Ireaд ran.

In fragments you have it,
so it is.

Ní h-ioncaoíḃ тura. Ní
h-eaд ran.

You are not to be trusted,
so you are not.

Cá ré зo дear aзaт. Тá
ran.

You have it in a nice way,
so you have.

Тá ré зo h-aınдeır aзaт.
Тá ran.

You have it in a mess,
so you have.

Зo h-aınдeır ireaд aтá
ré aзaт. Ireaд ran.

In a mess is how you have
it, so it is.

Ir тura a ḃuır é.

It was you that broke it.

Ní mé aċт Тaдз.

No, but Thade.

Le carúṗ ireaд ḃuır ré é.

It was with a hammer he
broke it.

Ní h-eaд aċт le тuaıз.

No, but with a hatchet.

Siné an carúṗ.

That is the hammer.

Sıдí an тuaз.

This is the hatchet.

Sıúд é Тaдз.

Yonder is Thade.

Siné é anran é.

There it is there.

Sıдé anro é.

Here it is here.

Sıúд é anrúд é.

There it is yonder.

Sıдí anro í.

Here she is here.

Sıní anran í.

There she is there.

Sıúд í anrúд í.

There she is yonder.

Тá ré anran.

It is there.

Тá ré anro.

It is here.

Tá ṛé anṛúv.	It is yonder.
Siné é.	That is it. That is he.
Sini í.	That is she. That is it.
Iṛeaḋ.	Yes. The matter is so.
Iṛeaḋ ṛan.	That matter is so.
Ní h-eaḋ.	No. The matter is not so.
Ní h-eaḋ ṛan.	That matter is not so.

*It will be seen from the above that é is the mascu-
line, or neuter, pronoun; that í is the feminine
pronoun; and that eaḋ is not a pronoun at all, but
a particle whose function it is to represent any de-
scription of* indefinite predication *after* iṛ. *Hence
eaḋ always represents the truth of some statement,
which* iṛ *asserts, and which* ní *denies.* Iṛeaḋ = " The
matter is so." Ní h-eaḋ = " The matter is not so."

Beiṫ.	The fact of being. To be.
Beiṫ láiviṛ.	To be strong.
Beiṫ laṡ.	To be weak.
Iṛ maiṫ an ṛuv beiṫ láiviṛ.	It is a good thing to be strong.
Iṛ olc an ṛuv beiṫ laṡ.	It is a bad thing to be weak.
B' ḟeáṛ liom beiṫ láiviṛ 'ná beiṫ laṡ.	I'd rather be strong than weak.
Caḋ 'na taoḃ ná ceanuiṡean tu bṛóṡa ḋuit ḟéin ?	Why don't you buy shoes for yourself?
Ṡan an t-aiṛṡeaḋ vo beiṫ aṡam.	Because I have not got the money.
Caḋ 'na taoḃ ná tuṡan tú leat an mála ?	Why do you not bring the bag?

é beit ró tron. | Because it is too heavy.
Cao 'na taob ná fuil ann-lan le o' cuio bío agat? | Why have you no kitchen with your food?
Ȝan aon fáȝail do beit aȝam air. | Because I have no means of getting it.
Cao cuiȝe ouit beit aȝ maȝaó fúm? | What are you making game of me for?
Ȝan aon ciall do beit aȝat. | Because you have no sense.
Cao 'na taob ná h-itean tú tuilleaó? | Why don't you eat more?
Mo óóitin do beit itte aȝam. | Because I have eaten enough.
An bfaȝaó beit irtiȝ uait? | Will you give me a night's lodging?
Ȝeabair, act ȝan beit 'ȝá inrint orm amárac. | I will, provided you will not be telling it to-morrow.
Ní fear beit aȝ caint air act ir ionȝantac an ouine tu! | There is no use in talking, you are an extraordinary person '
Ní fear beit aȝ caint air, do buaió an lá inoiu ar a bfeaca riam! | There is no use in talking, this day flogs all I have ever seen!
Ní 'l aon mait ouit beit liom! | There is no use in your being at me!
Ní h-ionan beit ar buile aȝur ar lán-buile. | There is a difference between being mad and being mad entirely.
Má'r mait leat beit buan cait fuar aȝur teit. | If you wish to live long take your food cold and run away.

Ɣan beiṫ am boṫṗaḋ iṗé ḃeanꝼaiṗ!
Not to be bothering me. 'tis what you'll do.

Tá ṗé ɣan beiṫ aṗ ꝼóɣnaṁ.
He is a little unwell.

Cuiḃṗaċ, ɣan beiṫ maoiṁteaċ.
Fairly well without much to boast of.

B' ꝼeaṗa ḋuit ɣan a ḃeiṫ aɣat aċt pṗáta aɣuṗ ɣṗáinne ṗalainn aꝺ tiɣ ꝼéin 'ná ꝺá mbeiḋeaḋ ṗóɣ aɣuṗ ṗóṗta aɣat i ꝺtiɣ an ꝼiṗ ṫall.
It would be better for you if you had but a potato and a grain of salt in your own house than if you had the greatest luxuries in another man's house.

Ꝺúḃaṗt leiṗ ɣan beiṫ aḃꝼaꝺ.
I told him not to be long (away).

Ꝺúḃaṗt leiṗ ɣan aon ꝺiṫneaṗ ꝺo ḃeiṫ aiṗ.
I told him not to be in any hurry.

Ꝺúḃaṗt leiṗ ɣan aon eaɣla ḃeiṫ aiṗ.
I told him not to be afraid.

Ꝺúḃaṗt leiṗ ɣan aon tṗuaɣ ḃeiṫ aiɣe ḋóiḃ.
I told him not to have any compassion for them.

Ꝺúḃaṗt leiṗ ɣan aon eaɣla ḃeiṫ aiɣe ṗómpa.
I told him not to be afraid of them.

Ꝺúḃaṗt leiṗ ɣan aon ḃeann ꝺo ḃeiṫ aiɣe oṗta.
I told him not to be influenced by them (not to mind them).

Ꝺúḃaṗt leiṗ ɣan aon ċall ꝺo ḃeiṫ aiɣe ċúca.
I told him not to have anything to do with them.

(*This* ċall *is a genuine Irish word. It does not mean the English word "call." The Irish for that is* ɣlaoḋ.

D

"Tugaſ mo ṡpeann mo
cáll 'ſ mo ſéaſc do
Séamuſ."

"I have given my affec-
tion, the *interest of my
mind* and my love, to
James."

"Ná bioḋ aon cáll aɡaꞇ
cuiɡe."

"Don't *interfere* with it."

It is very ridiculous for people who have learned a
LITTLE *Irish to proceed at once to* "CORRECT" *the
forms of speech which the best intellect of the nation
has been using for centuries, and to* REJECT *beautiful
Irish words because they happen to sound like certain
English words, with the meaning of which they have
no connection.)*

Iſ ſeáſ beiꞇ díomaoin
'ná ꞁoꞁoc ɡnóꞇac.

It is better to be idle than
doing bad work.

"Ceaꞇſaſ cailleac ɡan beiꞇ mannꞇac;
Ceaꞇſaſ Fſancac ɡan beiꞇ buiḋe;
Ceaꞇſaſ ɡſéaſaiḋe ɡan beiꞇ bſéaɡac;
'Sin dáſꞁéaɡ ná ſuil ſa ꞇíſ."

" Four old hags who are not gap-toothed :
Four Frenchmen who are not yellow ;
Four shoemakers who do not tell lies ;
There is a dozen people who do not exist in the
country."

END OF PART I.

APPENDIX.

Na h-Uiṁpeaċa.

Irish Numerals.

The Irish number has three different shapes in the mind. First, it is a substantive. Like any other substantive, it stands either with or without the definite article. With the definite article it means some *definite* number; as an ꞇ-aon = "the one," an ꝺeiċ = "the ten," an ċéaꝺ ꝺeiċ = "the first ten," an ꝺara cúiᵹ = "the second five." Without the definite article it is an *indefinite* substantive, cúiᵹ = "*a* five," ꝺeiċ = "*a* ten."

Secondly, in the Irish mind the idea of number is a *mental instrument for counting.* Then it has in speech the particle a before it. A h-aon = "one," a ꝺó = "two," a ꞇʀí = "three."

Every number, *when thus used as a counter,* has this particle before it. In counting, people have the habit of dropping, at certain numbers, from the second shape of the idea to the first, just as if, in English counting, a person were to say instead of "twelve," "a dozen," or instead of "twenty," "a score."

This alternation of the Irish mind, between the two shapes of the idea, gave rise to some confusion among scholars. They thought some of the Irish numbers *took* the particle and that others *did not*. The truth is that *none* of them take it when used as independent substantives, and that they *all* take it when used as counters. I have heard ᴀ céᴀᴅ used as a counter. It means *the last individual of the hundred*, whereas céᴀᴅ means the *whole hundred individuals*.

The third shape of the idea is that of a counter *in the form of an adjective*, i.e., "one horse," "two horses," "three horses," etc. In this method of Irish counting the first number is never used at all. We never say in Irish "*one* horse." We always say, cᴀpᴀl, ᴅᴀ cᴀpᴀl, ᴛʃí cᴀpᴀil, ceiᴛʃe cᴀpᴀil, etc.: beᴀn, ᴅᴀ ṁnᴀoí, ᴛʃí mnᴀ́, ceiᴛʃe mnᴀ́, etc.

Sometimes, in Irish counting, the individuals are kept so distinct as *never to constitute a plural*.

Cᴀpᴀl = one horse.

ᴅᴀ cᴀpᴀl = two horses.

ᴛʃí cᴀpᴀl = three horses.

Ceiᴛʃe cᴀpᴀl = four horses, etc.

Seᴀcᴛ, ocᴛ, and nᴀoi prefer the plural.

Thus the mystery of ʃíce cᴀpᴀl is easily seen through.

In the case of *verbal nouns* even ʃeᴀcᴛ, ocᴛ, and nᴀoi take the singular.

Seᴀcᴛ mbuᴀlᴀᴅ = seven thrashings.

Ocᴛ mbuᴀlᴀᴅ = eight thrashings.

Ɲᴀoi mbuᴀlᴀᴅ = nine thrashings.

ᴅeic mbuᴀlᴀᴅ = ten thrashings

Cúiᵹ beiʃbᴀᴅ = five boilings.

ᴛʃí ᴛʃiomúᵹᴀᴅ = three dryings.

ᴅᴀ ᴘᴀʃᵹᴀᴅ = two squeezings.

Cimilᴛ = (one) rubbing.

The learner must take care not to be misled by the grammars and their Latin terminologies. Those Latin terminologies do not fit our Irish language. They are all confusion.

ná h-uiṁreaċa.
IRISH NUMERALS.

an uiṁir féin.	THE NUMBER ITSELF.	
Aon.	One	(the number)
Dó.	Two	„
Trí.	Three	„
Ceaṫair.	Four	
Cúig.	Five	
Sé.	Six	„
Seaċt.	Seven	„
Oċt.	Eight	„
Naoi.	Nine	
Deiċ.	Ten	„
Aoinoéag.	Eleven	„
Dóoéag.	Twelve	„
Tríoéag.	Thirteen	
Ceaṫairoéag.	Fourteen	„
Cúigoéag.	Fifteen	„
Séioéag.	Sixteen	„
Seaċtoéag.	Seventeen	„
Oċtoéag.	Eighteen	„
Naoioéag.	Nineteen	„
Fiċe.	Twenty	„
Aon a'r fiċe.	Twenty-one	„
Dó a'r fiċe.	Twenty-two	„
Ceaṫair a'r fiċe	Twenty-four	„
⁊c. ⁊c.	&c.	
Deiċ a'r fiċe.	Thirty	„
Daċaḋ.	Forty	

This form of the numeral is a substantive and can have the definite article before it when the sense of the language so requires ; thus :—

An t-аоn.	The one.
An оó.	The two, *i.e.*, that individual *two*.
An tрí.	The three.
An ceаtаıр.	The four, *i.e.*, there is question of a number of fours and this is a certain one of them. It is the *four* of which mention has been made somewhere.

an uıṁır аɡ cóṁreаṁ.	THE NUMBER, COUNTING.
А h-аоn.	One.
А оó.	Two.
А tрí.	Three.
А ceаtаıр.	Four.
А cúıɡ.	Five.
А ré.	Six.
А reаċt.	Seven.
А h-oċt.	Eight.
А nаoı.	Nine.
А оeıċ.	Ten.
А h-аoınоéаɡ.	Eleven.
А оóoéаɡ.	Twelve.
А tрíоéаɡ.	Thirteen.
А ceаtаıроéаɡ.	Fourteen.
А cúıɡоéаɡ.	Fifteen.
А réıоéаɡ.	Sixteen.

ᴀ ρeᴀċᴅéᴀꝯ.	Seventeen.
ᴀ h-oċᴅéᴀꝯ.	Eighteen.
ᴀ naoιᴅéᴀꝯ.	Nineteen.
ᴀ ꝼιċe.	Twenty.
ᴀ h-ᴀon ᴀ’ρ ꝼιċe.	Twenty-one.
ᴀ ᴄρí ᴀ’ρ ꝼιċe.	Twenty-three.
ᴀ cúιꝯ ᴀ’ρ ꝼιċe.	Twenty-five.
ᴀ ᴅeιċ ᴀ’ρ ꝼιċe.	Thirty.
ᴀ ᴅᴀċᴀᴅ.	Forty.
ᴀ h-ᴀon ᴀ’ρ ᴅᴀċᴀᴅ.	Forty-one.

This form of numeral is used while the finger of the person counting points, for each numeral, to the individual which is counted. The ᴀ is not repeated in the compound forms. It would be impossible to repeat it. No individual thing could occupy the position both of ᴀ ᴅeιċ and ᴀ ꝼιċe, for example. Hence a thing could not be ᴀ ᴅeιċ ᴀ’ρ ᴀ ꝼιċe. It must be ᴀ ᴅeιċ ᴀ’ρ ꝼιċe.

ᴀn uιṁιρ ᴀꝯ Léιριúꝯᴀᴅ.	THE NUMBER, DEFINING SOMETHING.
ᴀn ᴄ-ᴀonṁᴀᴅ Lá. / ᴀn ċéᴀᴅ Lá.	The first day.
ᴀn ᴅóṁᴀᴅ Lá. / ᴀn ᴅᴀρᴀ Lá.	The second day.
ᴀn ᴄρíṁᴀᴅ Lá. / ᴀn ᴄρeᴀρ Lá.	The third day.
ᴀn ceᴀᴄρṁᴀᴅ Lá.	The fourth day.
ᴀn cúιꝯṁᴀᴅ Lá.	The fifth day.
ᴀn ρéṁᴀᴅ La.	The sixth day.
ᴀn ρeᴀċᴄṁᴀᴅ Lá.	The seventh day.

An t-oċtṁaḋ lá.	The eighth day.
An naomaḋ lá.	The ninth day.
An ueiċṁaḋ lá.	The tenth day.
(An ueaċṁaḋ.	The tithe.)
An t-aonṁaḋ lá ḋéag.	The eleventh day.
An ḋara lá ḋéag.	The twelfth day.
An tríṁaḋ lá ḋéag.	The thirteenth day.
An ceaṫṁaḋ lá ḋéag.	The fourteenth day.
An cúigṁaḋ lá ḋéag.	The fifteenth day.
An séṁaḋ lá ḋéag.	The sixteenth day.
An seaċtṁaḋ lá ḋéag.	The seventeenth day.
An t-oċtṁaḋ lá ḋéag.	The eighteenth day.
An naomaḋ lá ḋéag.	The nineteenth day.
An fiċṁaḋ lá.	The twentieth day.
An t-aonṁaḋ lá fiċiu.	The twenty-first day.
An ḋara lá fiċiu. ⎫ An ḋóṁaḋ lá fiċiu. ⎭	The twenty-second day.
An tríṁaḋ lá fiċiu.	The twenty-third day.
An ceaṫṁaḋ lá fiċiu.	The twenty-fourth day.
An cúigṁaḋ lá fiċiu.	The twenty-fifth day.
An séṁaḋ lá fiċiu.	The twenty-sixth day.
An ueiċṁaḋ lá fiċiu.	The thirtieth day.
An t-aonṁaḋ lá ḋéag ar fiċiu.	The thirty-first day.
An ḋara lá ḋéag ar fiċiu.	The thirty-second day.
An tríṁaḋ lá ḋéag ar fiċiu.	The thirty-third day.
An ceaṫṁaḋ lá ḋéag ar fiċiu.	The thirty-fourth day.
An uaċaomaḋ lá. ⎫ Lá a ḋaċaiu. ⎭	The fortieth day.

"ı mbliaʒaın a ʊaċaıʊ beıʊ aıcıon ʒan ŗíol ʒan blác."	"In the year 1840 furze will be without seed and without blossom."

This word "ʊaċaıʊ" should not be writen ʊá ŗıċıʊ. What the people have said for centuries is ʊaċaıʊ. The derivation, of course, is ʊá ŗıċıʊ. But what sort of *English* would we have if instead of the *word* we were to write its *derivation* !

An c-aonṁaʊ lá a'ŗ ʊaċaʊ.	The forty-first day.
An ʊaŗa lá a'ŗ ʊaċaʊ·	The forty-second day.
An cŗíṁaʊ lá a'ŗ ʊaċaʊ.	The forty-third day.
An ʊeıċṁaʊ lá a'ŗ ʊaċaʊ.	The fiftieth day.
An c-aonṁaʊ lá ʊéaʒ a'ŗ ʊaċaʊ.	The fifty-first day.
An ʊaŗa la ʊéaʒ a'ŗ ʊaċaʊ.	The fifty-second day.
Lá a cŗí ŗıċıʊ.	The sixtieth day.
bliaʒaın a cŗí ŗıċıʊ.	The year '60.
bliaʒaın a ċeıcŗe ŗıċıʊ.	The eightieth year.
An c-aonṁaʊ bliaʒaın a'ŗ ċeıcŗe ŗıċıʊ.	The eighty-first year.
An ʊeıċṁaʊ bliaʒaın a'ŗ ċeıcŗe ŗıċıʊ.	The ninetieth year.
An c-aonṁaʊ bliaʒaın ʊéaʒ a'ŗ ċeıcŗe ŗıċıʊ.	The ninety-first year
An céaʊṁaʊ bliaʒaın.	The hundredth year.
An c-aonṁaʊ bliaʒaın aʒuŗ céaʊ.	The hundred-and-first year.

All these expressions are exactly as I have heard them from the mouths of the people.

DAOINE D'Á gCÓṀREAṀ.	PERSONS BEING COUNTED.
Duine.	A person.
Beirt	Two persons.
Triúr.	Three persons.
Ceaṫrar.	Four persons.
Cúigear.	Five persons.
Seisear.	Six persons.
Mórṡeisear.	Seven persons.
Oċtar.	Eight persons.
Naonḃúr.	Nine persons.
Deiċniúḃur.	Ten persons.
Aoinne déag.	Eleven persons.
Ḋáréag.	Twelve persons.
Trí ḋuine ḋéag.	Thirteen persons.
Ceiṫre ḋuine ḋéag.	Fourteen persons.
Cuig ḋuine ḋéag.	Fifteen persons.
Sé duine ḋéag.	Sixteen persons.
Seaċt nduine ḋéag.	Seventeen persons.
Oċt nduine ḋéag.	Eighteen persons.
Naoi ḋuine ḋéag.	Nineteen persons.
Fiċe duine.	Twenty persons.
Duine agus fiċe.	Twenty-one persons.
Beirt a's fiċe.	Twenty-two persons.
Daċad duine.	Forty persons.
Duine agus daċad.	Forty-one persons.
Deiċ nduine agus daċad. Deiċniúḃúr a's daċad.	Fifty persons.
Trí fiċid duine.	Sixty persons.
Duine agus trí fiċid.	Sixty-one persons.

Ueiṗc a'ṗ cṗí ṗíċıo.	Sixty-two persons.
Oeıċnıúḃuṗ a'ṗ cṗí ṗíċıo.	Seventy persons.
Aoınne oéaʒ a'ṗ cṗí ṗíċıo.	Seventy-one persons.
Oáṗéaʒ a'ṗ cṗí ṗíċıo.	Seventy-two persons.
Cṗí ḃuıne oeaʒ a'ṗ cṗí ṗíċıo.	Seventy-three persons.
Cèıcṗe ṗíċıo ouıne.	Eighty persons.
Ouıne aʒuṗ ċeıcṗe ṗíċıo.	Eighty-one persons.
Occaṗ a'ṗ ċeıcṗe ṗíċıo.	Eighty-eight persons.
Oeıċnıúḃuṗ a'ṗ ċeıcṗe ṗíċıo.	Ninety persons.
Aoınne oéaʒ a'ṗ ċeıcṗe ṗíċıo.	Ninety-one persons.
Oáṗéaʒ aʒuṗ ċeıcṗe ṗíċıo.	Ninety-two persons.
Cṗí ḃuıne oéaʒ a'ṗ ċeıcṗe ṗíċıo.	Ninety-three persons.

The ṗ in oáṗéaʒ is broad. There *was* a o between it and the é.

Céao ouıne.	One hundred persons.
Ouıne aʒuṗ céao.	One hundred and one persons.
Ueıṗc aʒuṗ céao.	One hundred and two persons.
Cṗıúṗ a'ṗ céao.	One hundred and three persons.
Ceacṗaṗ a'ṗ céao.	One hundred and four persons.
Cúıʒeaṗ a'ṗ céao.	One hundred and five persons.

Oeicṁúḃuṗ a'ṡ céaᴅ.	One hundred and ten persons.
Mìle ᴅuıne.	One thousand persons.
Céaᴅ aᵹuṡ mìle ᴅuıne.	One thousand one hundred persons.
Céaᴅ mìle ᴅuıne.	One hundred thousand persons.
Ouıne aᵹuṡ céaᴅ mìle.	One hundred thousand and one persons.
Ouıne aᵹuṡ mìle.	One thousand and one persons.
Oeıċ céaᴅ mìle ᴅuıne.	One million of persons.
Ouıne aᵹuṡ ᴅeıċ céaᴅ mìle.	One million and one persons.
Fìċe céaᴅ mìle ᴅuıne.	2,000,000 persons.
Ouıne aᵹuṡ fìċe céaᴅ mìle.	2,000,001 persons.
Ƅeıṗc aᵹuṡ fìċe céaᴅ mìle.	2,000,002 persons.
Céaᴅ aᵹuṡ fìċe céaᴅ mìle ᴅuıne.	2,000,100 persons.
Mìle aᵹuṡ fìċe céaᴅ mìle ᴅuıne.	2,001,000 persons.
Oeıċ mìle aᵹuṡ fìċe céaᴅ mìle ᴅuıne.	2,010,000 persons.
Céaᴅ mìle aᵹuṡ fìċe céaᴅ mìle ᴅuıne.	2,100,000 persons.
Oeıċ céaᴅ mìle aᵹuṡ fìċe céaᴅ mìle ᴅuıne.	3,000,000 persons.
Oaċaᴅ céaᴅ mìle ᴅuıne,	4,000,000 persons.
Cṗì fıċıᴅ céaᴅ mìle ᴅuıne.	6,000,000 persons.

Céitṗe ṗiċiᴅ céaᴅ míle ᴅuine.	8,000,000 persons.
Céaᴅ céaᴅ míle ᴅuine.	10,000,000 persons.
Míle míle ᴅuine.	1,000,000 persons.
Céaᴅ míle míle ᴅuine.	100,000,000 persons.
ᴅeiċ céaᴅ míle míle ᴅuine.	1,000,000,000 persons.
ᴅuine aᵹuṗ ᴅeiċ céaᴅ míle míle.	1,000,000,001 persons.

neiċe ᴅ'á ᵹcóṁṗeaṁ.	THINGS BEING COUNTED.
Cloċ ṁine.	A stone of meal.
ᴅá ċloiċ ṁine.	Two stone of meal.
Tṗí cloċa mine.	Three stone of meal.
Ceitṗe cloċa mine.	Four stone of meal.
Cúiᵹ cloċa mine.	Five stone of meal.
Sé cloċa mine.	Six stone of meal.
Seaċt cloċa mine.	Seven stone of meal.
Oċt cloċa mine.	Eight stone of meal.
Naoi ᵹcloċa mine.	Nine stone of meal.
ᴅeiċ cloċa mine.	Ten stone of meal.
aon ċloċ ᴅéaᵹ mine.	Eleven stone of meal.
ᴅá ċloiċ ᴅéaᵹ ṁine. ᴅá ċloiċ ᴅéaᵹ mine.	Twelve stone of meal.
Tṗí cloċa ᴅéaᵹ mine.	Thirteen stone of meal.
Naoi ᵹcloċa ᴅéaᵹ mine.	Nineteen stone of meal.
Fiċe cloċ ṁine. Fiċe cloċ mine.	Twenty stone of meal.
Cloċ aᵹuṗ fiċe mine.	Twenty-one stone of meal.
ᴅá ċloiċ a'ṗ fiċe mine.	Twenty-two stone of meal.
Tṗí cloċa ṗiċiᴅ mine.	Twenty-three stone of meal.
Ceitṗe cloċa ṗiċiᴅ mine.	Twenty-four stone of meal.
Naoi ᵹcloċa ṗiċiᴅ mine.	Twenty-nine stone of meal.

Ðeic cloca ficio mine.	Thirty stone of meal.
Aon cloc ðéaᵹ aᵦ ficio mine.	Thirty-one stone of meal.
Ðá cloic ðéaᵹ aᵦ ficio mine.	Thirty-two stone of meal.
Tᵦí cloca ðéaᵹ aᵦ ficio mine.	Thirty-three stone of meal
Ðaca�at cloc mine.⎫ Ðaca�at cloc mine.⎭	Forty stone of meal.

The learner will perceive that in one of these phrases the m of mine is aspirated, in the other it is not. Here is the reason. If ðaca�t cloc be taken as *one thing*, it is a phrase-noun and *not* feminine. If the words be taken *singly*, then the word cloc aspirates mine because the word cloc is feminine. The speaker is at perfect liberty to say ðacaᵗ .... cloc-mine, or ðacaᵗ-cloc ... mine. This different grouping of the words is of course made merely in the mind. It need not be expressed by the voice.

WITH THE DEFINITE ARTICLE.

An cloc mine.	The stone of meal.
An ðá cloic mine.	The two stone of meal.
Na tᵦí cloca mine.	The three stone of meal.
An t-aon cloc ðéaᵹ mine.	The eleven stone of meal.
An ðá cloic ðéaᵹ mine.	The twelve stone of meal.
Na tᵦí cloca ðeaᵹ mine.	The thirteen stone of meal
Na naoi ᵹcloca ðéaᵹ mine.	The nineteen stone of meal
An fice cloc mine.⎫ An fice cloc mine.⎭	The twenty stone of meal

An cloc aṛ fiċio mine.	The twenty-one stone of meal.
An oá cloiċ aṛ fiċio mine.	The twenty-two stone of meal.
Ila cṛí clocá fiċio mine.	The twenty-three stone of meal.
An c-aon cloc oéaʒ aṛ fiċio mine.	The thirty-one stone of meal.
An oá cloiċ oéaʒ aṛ fiċio mine.	The thirty-two stone of meal.
Ila cṛí clocá oéaʒ aṛ fiċio mine.	The thirty-three stone of meal.
An oaċao cloc mine. ⎫ An oaċao cloc mine. ⎭	The forty stone of meal.
An cloc a'ṛ oaċao mine.	The forty-one stone of meal.
An oá cloiċ a'ṛ oaċao mine.	The forty-two stone of meal.
Ila cṛí clocá a'ṛ oaċao mine.	The forty-three stone of meal.
An cṛí fiċio cloc mine. An cṛí fiċio cloc mine. ⎫ c. ⎭	The sixty stone of meal, &c.
Oá ṛʒiling aṛ cloiċ mine.	Two shillings for a stone of meal.
Oá ṛʒiling aṛ oá cloiċ mine.	Two shillings for two stone of meal.
Oá ṛʒiling aṛ cṛí clocá mine.	Two shillings for three stone of meal.

I have never heard clocáiḃ in these constructions. It seems to me that grammarians are utterly ignorant of the true meaning of this -ıb which they are pleased to call "*dative plural.*" Now, in the above example if the τρί cloċᴀ did not mean a given *single* measure if it meant three *individual things*, it should be cloċᴀıb. Here τρí cloċᴀ is *one* collective quantity, and it is that fact, before my mind, which prevents me from saying cloċᴀıb. It appears then that this -ıb expresses, not a difference of *case*, but a difference of *mode*. There is far more purity of language in the speech of the people than there is in our grammars. We have no *Irish* grammar. They are all *Latin* grammars.

Leᴀt nᴀ cloıċe mıne.	Half of the stone of meal.
Leᴀt ᴀn ᴅᴀ́ ċloċ mine.	Half of the two stone of meal.
Leᴀt ᴀn ᴅᴀ́ ċloċ mıne.	
Leᴀt nᴀ ᴅτρí ᵹcloċ mıne.	Half of the three stone of meal.
Leᴀt nᴀ nᴅeıċ ᵹcloċ mıne.	Half of the ten stone of meal.
Leᴀt ᴀn ᴀon ċloċ ᴅéᴀᵹ mıne.	Half of the eleven stone of meal.
Leᴀt ᴀn ᴅᴀ́ ċloċ ᴅéᴀᵹ mıne.	Half of the twelve stone of meal.
Leᴀt nᴀ ᴅτρí ᵹcloċ nᴅéᴀᵹ mıne.	Half of the thirteen stone of meal.
Leᴀt ᴀn ᴘ́ıċeᴀᴅ cloċ mıne.	Half of the twenty stone of meal.
Leᴀt ᴀn ᴀon ċloċ ᴀρ ᴘ́ıċıᴅ mıne.	Half of the twenty-one stone of meal.
Leᴀt ᴀn ᴅᴀ́ ċloċ ᴀρ ᴘ́ıċıᴅ mıne.	Half of the twenty-two stone of meal.

Leᴀᴄ nᴀ ᴅᴄᴘí ᵹᴄloᴄ ᴀᴘ ᵽíᴄíᴅ mine.	Half of the twenty-three stone of meal.
Leᴀᴄ ᴀn ᴅᴀᴄᴀᴅ cloᴄ mine	Half of the forty stone of meal.
Uᴀᴘ; ᴀon uᴀᴘ ᴀᵯᴀin.	Once.
Ᵹᴀ uᴀᴘ; ᵽᴀoí ᴅó.	Twice.
Cᴘí h-uᴀᴘe; ᵽó ᴄᴘí.	Three times.
Ceicᴘe h-uᴀᴘe; ᵽó ᴄeᴀ-ᴄᴀᴘ.	Four times.
Ᵹeiᴄ n-uᴀᴘe; ᵽó ᴅeiᴄ.	Ten times.
ᵽíᴄe uᴀᴘ.	Twenty times.
Uᴀᴘ um ᴀ ᴘeᴀᴄ.	At odd times, now and then, "a seldom time."
Seᴀᴄᴄ n-uᴀᴘe ᴅéᴀᵹ ᴀᴘ ᵽíᴄíᴅ.	"Hundreds of times."

When uᴀᴘ signifies "an hour" it has always the words "ᴀ' ᴄloiᵹ" with it. Sometimes, especially in the case of verbal nouns, the *individuals counted* are kept so distinct in the mind as never to constitute a plural, no matter how large their number.

Cᴀᴘᴀᴅ.	A twist or turn.
Ᵹᴀ ᴄᴀᴘᴀᴅ.	Two twistings.
Cᴘí ᴄᴀᴘᴀᴅ.	Three twistings
Ceicᴘe ᴄᴀᴘᴀᴅ.	Four twistings.
Cúiᵹ ᴄᴀᴘᴀᴅ.	Five twistings.
Sé ᴄᴀᴘᴀᴅ.	Six twistings.
Seᴀᴄᴄ ᵹᴄᴀᴘᴀᴅ.	Seven twistings
Oᴄᴄ ᵹᴄᴀᴘᴀᴅ,	Eight twistings
Ꮨᴀoí ᵹᴄᴀᴘᴀᴅ.	Nine twistings.
Ᵹeiᴄ ᵹᴄᴀᴘᴀᴅ.	Ten twistings

E

Aon ċasaḋ ḋéag.	Eleven twistings.
Trí ċasaḋ ḋéag.	Thirteen twistings.
Fiċe casaḋ.	Twenty twistings.
Céad casaḋ.	A hundred twistings.
Ḃaineamair trí ċasaḋ ḋéag ar ḟiċid ar an mada ruaḋ.	We turned the fox around thirty-three times.

Sometimes, for the purpose of smoothness, the word ceann is introduced in counting.

Bó.	One cow.
Ḋá bó.	Two cows.
Trí cinn ḋe ḃuaiḃ.	Three cows. / Three head of cattle.
Ceiṫre cinn ḋe ḃuaiḃ.	Four head of cattle.
Aon ċeannḋéag ḋe ḃuaiḃ.	Eleven cows.
Naoi gcinn ḋéag ḋe ḃuaiḃ.	Nineteen cows.
Fiċe bó.	Twenty cows.
Féur bó.	The grass of a cow.
Féur ḋá bó.	The grass of two cows.
Féur trí cinn ḋe ḃuaiḃ.	The grass of three cows.
Féur trí mbó.	The grass of three cows.
Féur ċeiṫre mbó. / Féur ceiṫre cinn ḋe ḃuaiḃ.	} The grass of four cows.
Féur ċúig mbó. / Féur cúig cinn ḋe ḃuaiḃ.	} The grass of five cows.
Féur deiċ mbó. / Féur deiċ cinn ḋe ḃuaiḃ.	} The grass of ten cows.

Féuṗ aon ċeann véaʒ ve   The grass of eleven cows.
ḃuaiḃ.

Aon ċeann veaʒ is a phrase noun and therefore *indeclinable.*

Féuṗ an aon ċeann
   véaʒ ve ḃuaiḃ.   } The grass of the eleven cows.
Féuṗ an aon ḃó véaʒ

Féuṗ an ficeav bó.   The grass of the twenty
                          cows.

Féuṗ na h-aon bó.   The grass of the one cow.
Féuṗ an aon ċapail.   The grass of the one horse.
Cion vuine.   One person's share.
Cion beiṗce.   Two persons' share.
Cion ṫṗíṗ.   Three persons' share.
Cion ceaṫṗaiṗ.   Four persons' share.
Cion na beiṗce.   The two persons' share.
Cion an ċúiʒiṗ.   The five persons' share.
Cion an aoinne véaʒ.   The eleven persons' share.
Cion an váṗéaʒ.   The twelve persons' share.
Feiṫm an váṗéaʒ.   As much as twelve persons
                          could do in one effort.

Cion fiċe vuine.   Twenty persons' share.
Cion vuine aʒuṗ fiċe.   Twenty-one persons' share.
Feiṫm fiċe vuine .   As much as twenty persons
                          could do in one effort.

Feiṫm céav capal.   The force of 100 horses, *i.e.,*
                          100 horse power.

www.ingramcontent.com/pod-product-compliance
Lightning Source LLC
Chambersburg PA
CBHW021517090426
42739CB00007B/662